# The Patterns of War
## through the
## Eighteenth Century

# The Patterns of War through the Eighteenth Century

LARRY H. ADDINGTON

INDIANA UNIVERSITY PRESS
*Bloomington and Indianapolis*

Manufactured in the United States of America

**Library of Congress Cataloging-in-Publication Data**

Addington, Larry H.
The patterns of war through the eighteenth century / Larry H.
Addington.
p.    cm.
Bibliography: p.
Includes index.
ISBN 0-253-30131-9.—ISBN 0-253-20551-4 (pbk.)
1. Military art and science—History.   2. Military history.
I. Title.
U27.A294    1990
355'.009—dc20                          89-45190
1 2 3 4 5    94 93 92 91 90              CIP

**For Theodore Ropp**
Mentor and Friend

# CONTENTS

# LIST OF ILLUSTRATIONS

# LIST OF MAPS

# PREFACE

This introductory study of the history of war and warfare is intended as a companion piece to my earlier work *The Patterns of War since the Eighteenth Century* (Indiana University Press, 1984). As in that work, my object was to write a brief history that suggests that much military and naval history may be usefully viewed in terms of patterns of war. I should explain at the outset that by "patterns" I mean the unique social-political, technological, and organizational factors in each period of history, which, at a given time, present (at least to my eye) a "pattern" or form. These patterns lie implicit in the narrative, but I have tried at intervals to highlight them for the reader. I have also tried to mention those patterns which seem to transcend more than one period, in particular tactical and logistical patterns, and thus perhaps make the reader more sensitive to how armies and navies performed in the periods addressed. At intervals I have discussed particular battles in some detail in order to give more life to the narrative and to suggest how the prevailing patterns of war affected military and naval behavior on particular occasions. Lack of space, however, made it impossible for me to discuss more than a few battles in detail. Still, given the nature of my theme, I think little would have been gained by adding more battlefield accounts.

I am a historian who is particularly resistant to the notion that the patterns mentioned above may be usefully examined in some abstract form outside the historical events in which they occurred. I have, therefore, tried to include enough political, social, and economic history that the student is encouraged to see that military development occurs not in isolation from the rest of the prevailing culture but, on the contrary, war is highly imprinted by the culture in which it takes place. In other words, I see war and warfare (the latter being the means and methods by which war is waged) as more of a historical phenomenon than a scientific one, one in which the "rules of the game" vary according to the culture and the time. Although there may be a "science" for waging war in a particular era and culture, it seems to me that no "principles of war," save those that are reducible to common sense, have ever existed independent of time and circumstance. Accordingly, perhaps one of the great values in studying military history is to sensitize ourselves to seek the peculiar qualities, and thereby arrive at a better understanding, of war in our time. I am also aware that very much more must be left out than included in a book of so few pages covering thousands of years, and I hope it will be clear from the narrative why I have paid most attention to the military cultures of the Near East and the Western world.

This book ends where the former work began, at the start of the era of the American and French revolutions, which are only briefly covered in connection with the Neoclassical period which preceded them. Those up-heavals profoundly changed the social-political nature of war in North America and in Europe, and they were followed by the Industrial Revolutions of the nineteenth and twentieth centuries which transformed the technology and in some respects the organization of war almost beyond recognition. Indeed, the patterns of war have undergone so many revolutionary changes over the last two centuries that it did not seem disproportionate to spend more pages in my previous book on those centuries than I have spent on all the preceding centuries in this one. Still, all products of civilization—and that, unfortunately, includes war as I have tried to make clear in the text—stand on the shoulders of those that preceded them. The more distant military and naval past may be studied to advantage in order to understand the patterns of war in our times, and with a perspective we may find nowhere else.

It should go without saying that any shortcomings or errors in this book are my responsibility, but I cannot conclude this preface without acknowledgment by name of some of the institutions and people who rendered me assistance in its research and writing. A fellowship from the Citadel Development Foundation was of great financial help, and for that assistance I wish to express my thanks. I also wish to thank John Gallman, Director of the Indiana University Press, for his willingness to publish and for many helpful suggestions; John Coussons, head of the history department at The Citadel, for trying to arrange schedules and course loads to assist me in finding time for research and writing; Clark G. Reynolds, professor of history at the College of Charleston and distinguished maritime historian, who took the time to read the final form of the manuscript and to offer helpful criticisms; Theodore Ropp, professor emeritus of Duke University, for his reading of the manuscript and his unfailing interest in the work of his former students; John W. Gordon, professor of military and naval history at The Citadel, whose ideas and observations about the manuscript and the patterns of war were very helpful; John Thomas, former assistant professor of ancient and medieval history at The Citadel, who kindly read and critiqued the first two chapters; and Gunther Rothenberg, professor of history at Purdue University, who read an early version of the manuscript and made useful suggestions for improvement. And I would be remiss not to mention the unfailing encouragement of Amanda, my wife, in this project as in all others.

# The Patterns of War
## through the
## Eighteenth Century

# ONE

■ ■ ■

# Ancient War before the Age of Rome

## I. Pre-Civilized War, 200,000–3200 B.C.

*Homo sapiens* ("knowing man") emerged in the Paleolithic (Old Stone) age, perhaps two hundred thousand years ago, and for tens of thousands of years thereafter humankind subsisted by hunting and gathering naturally occurring fruits, grains, and vegetables. The communities of the Old Stone age were the migratory family, clan, and tribe, and their weapons were the club, the stone axe, the spear (a thrusting weapon), the javelin (a throwing weapon), and the wooden bow and arrow. The earliest Old Stone age bows were made of a single piece of wood, but the more powerful compound bow, made of several layers of wood bound together, also appeared in the later Old Stone age. Although our knowledge of Paleolithic warfare is largely conjectural (few artifacts have survived from that time), presumably small rival groups fought each other for possession of caves, water holes, food, and possibly women, but only a few cave drawings represent primitive men engaged in what may have been combat. Judging from the drawings, Paleolithic men spent far more time on the hunt than fighting among themselves.

The Neolithic or New Stone age began about 7000 B.C. in the Near East, just north of Mesopotamia (meaning literally the land "between two rivers," the Tigris and Euphrates), and was characterized by the building of stone or mud-brick dwellings in permanent villages, the domestication of animals, and the sowing and reaping of grain. Besides producing pottery, weaving textiles, and raising shrines to their gods, Neolithic people built earthen, brick, or stone walls around their communities, presumably for defense, which is perhaps an indication that combativeness among different groups of mankind was becoming more common. Land that could be cultivated, fixed abodes, and valuable personal possessions were worth fighting for, and probably all able-bodied adult males in a community were expected to take up arms to defend it or to join in the attack on communities of rivals. Thus, the warrior host or militia, simply a group of armed men fielded by a community in a temporary capacity, became the first recognizable form of military organization.

About 4500 B.C., artisans in Mesopotamia discovered how to extract copper from oxide ores by heating them with charcoal, and a little later they learned how to extract tin. But both copper and tin were too soft for the making of satisfactory weapons, which continued to be made of wood and stone until about 3200 B.C. Then Mesopotamian artisans opened a new age of warfare with the discovery that by adding tin to copper they could create a metal alloy, bronze, that was stronger than either copper or tin. Bronze was suitable for the making of blades for daggers, heads for battle axes and maces, and points for spears, javelins, and arrows. Being a relatively light metal, bronze was also suited for the making of helmets, shields, and armor protection for the torso. Scale armor, the earliest torso protection made with bronze, was created by sewing overlapping pieces of bronze to a fabric backing. The principal shock weapons (weapons designed to be wielded in the hand for cutting, stabbing, or bludgeoning) in the Bronze Age were the short-bladed dagger, the battle-axe, the spear, the mace, and a sickle-like sword with a long handle and a relatively short blade. Long-bladed swords awaited metallurgical discoveries whereby iron could be tempered to a steel-like strength.

## II. Warfare in the Near East, 3200–500 B.C.

### A. Warfare in the Bronze Age

Civilization (living in cities) commenced in the Near East shortly before 3000 B.C. with the founding of Sumer, near the head of the Persian Gulf and in territory that is now part of Iraq. Akkad was founded slightly later and further north in Mesopotamia. The Sumerians and Akkadians inhabited small, walled cities, and surviving artifacts suggest that as early as 3000 B.C. they waged a relatively sophisticated warfare. A surviving stone carving from Sumer depicts Sumerian soldiers massed in a phalanx (i.e., a close formation several ranks deep), each soldier armed with a spear and protected by a helmet and a cape studded with metal disks. Other archaeological evidence suggests that the Sumerian armies may have been the first to employ the war chariot, although down to 1500 B.C. war chariots in the Near East were drawn by donkeys and onagers rather than horses. Cavalry (i.e., soldiers who fought from horseback) did not become common until after 1000 B.C., and they did not have stirrups throughout the ancient period. The Akkadian methods of war were similar to the Sumerian except the Akkadians may have invented the composite bow, a complex machine made of wood, animal horn, sinews, tendons, and glue, that was more powerful than either the simple or the compound bow.

What is most striking about the armories of these earliest known civilizations is that they possessed nearly all the kinds of basic weapons known to the ancient world for thousands of years. With the exception of the

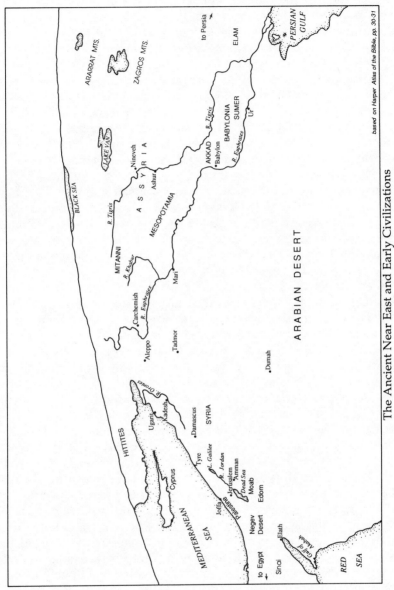

The Ancient Near East and Early Civilizations

based on Harper Atlas of the Bible, pp. 30-31

catapult and the *ballista* (a kingsized siege bow), and the long-bladed iron sword, later weapons in the ancient period were merely technical improvements on the prototypes of 3000 B.C.

Unfortunately, we know very little in detail about the campaigns and battles of the early civilizations until after 1300 B.C. We do know that under King Sargon I (2370–2315 B.C.) the Akkadians conquered the Sumerians and united the territories of Akkad and Sumer, and that the Akkadian-Sumerian empire weakened under the attacks of the Elamites of western Iran and the Amorites of the Arabian desert. By 1760 B.C. the Amorites had conquered the whole of Mesopotamia, and the Amorite king Hammurabi (1792–1759 B.C.), famous as the "Law Giver," established a capital at Babylon. The Babylonians maintained their domination of Mesopotamia until 1595 B.C., when the Hittites, a people who, unlike the semitic Akkadians and Babylonians, spoke an Indo-European language, swept out of Anatolia (a territory now in Turkey) to raid Mesopotamia repeatedly. Although Babylonia survived the Hittite raids, it was so weakened by them that it eventually succumbed to the invasions of the Aramaeans from Syria and to the military rivalry of Assyria, a civilization developing around the city of Ashur on the upper Tigris.

We also know that Egypt, another great center of early civilization, developed along the Nile river in northeast Africa, and was originally divided into separate kingdoms. Shortly before 3000 B.C., these kingdoms were united under a single monarchy, and the subsequent eras of the Old Kingdom and Middle Kingdom saw pyramid building, the establishment of the pharaoh as a god-king, and the development of centralized administration. The Egyptians did not adopt the war chariot until 1,500 years after it originated in Mesopotamia and only after it was introduced to them by the Hyksos, a people from the Sinai desert who swept over the Nile delta in 1670 B.C. and ruled over much of Egypt for over a century.

Only after the expulsion of the Hyksos and the advent of the New Kingdom was Egypt able to make an undisputed mark on military history. Then Pharaoh Thutmose III (1490–1436 B.C.)—sometimes called the "Napoleon of Egypt"—led his army in no fewer than fifteen successful campaigns. Under Pharaoh Amenhotep III (1398–1361 B.C.), the New Kingdom reached its imperial zenith when it controlled Nubia (the Sudan), Canaan (now in modern Israel), Syria, and much of Mesopotamia. At least by Amenhotep III's time, if not before, the pharaoh was served by a regular, or professional, army that also included foreign mercenaries, and these professional forces were supplemented by militia as needed. The advent of civilization had reached the point, in the case of Egypt, where specialization of labor was reflected in its military efforts.

In the next century, Egypt and the Hittite empire in Anatolia repeatedly clashed, the Hittite kings encouraging Egypt's client rulers in Canaan and Syria to rebel against Egypt's dominion. One such rebellion led to an Egyptian invasion of Syria under Pharaoh Ramses II and to the battle of Kadesh on the Orontes river in 1288 B.C. Thanks to an ancient memorial to Ramses II which has survived to our time, the battle of Kadesh is the first battle of the Bronze Age in the Near East of which we have much tactical knowledge.

### B. The Battle of Kadesh

According to the Egyptian account, Ramses II personally commanded the Egyptian army that marched by an inland route from Lebanon into Syria. It numbered perhaps twenty thousand men and was divided into four divisions, respectively designated as Amon, Re, Ptah, and Seth in honor of the Egyptian deities. An elite force of Canaanite mercenaries, perhaps 5,000 strong called the Ne'arim (literally "young men"), marched independently of the main force by a coastal route with orders to link up with the main army around Kadesh. Each of these divisions and the Ne'arim included war chariots drawn by horses, and the infantry of each was divided between spearmen and archers, the latter armed with the excellent Egyptian composite bow. The smallest tactical unit among the infantry was roughly equivalent in size to a company in an army of today. The infantry companies normally marched in a formation of ten files and twenty ranks, and by simply facing right or left, the company could be drawn up in a battle formation.

As his army was approaching Kadesh, Ramses II was tricked by information planted by the Hittites into believing that the Hittite army, which also included Canaanite soldiers and numbered perhaps 16,000 men, had withdrawn further north to the vicinity of Aleppo. In reality, it lay hidden beyond the river Orontes near Kadesh, awaiting a favorable moment to attack Ramses's army when it should arrive. Unaware of the danger, Ramses, the royal retinue, and the division called Amon went into camp near Kadesh and awaited the arrival of the other divisions and the Ne'arim from the coast. Re, the second of the Egyptian divisions in the line of march, was just opposite the concealed Hittite forces and less than a mile from Ramses II's camp when the Hittites made their move.

Led by 2,500 war chariots (each carrying three soldiers, two of whom were armed with spears) and crossing the Orontes by the fords, the Hittite attack caught Re by surprise and soon sent its men into flight. The Hittites then refocused their efforts on the camp of Amon, secure in the knowledge that the Egyptian divisions of Ptah and Seth were too far distant to intervene. Although Amon put up a more determined resistance than Re, it too was defeated and forced to flee. But then the Hittites blundered. They delayed their pursuit in order to loot the Egyptian camp, and in the meanwhile the Ne'arim, the elite force marching from the coast, arrived on the scene. Under Ramses II's leadership, the Ne'arim counter-attacked with such vigor that the surprised Hittites were driven out of the camp of Amon and against the Orontes, and apparently many Hittite and Canaanite soldiers were killed as they tried to escape across the river. Ramses II's victory at Kadesh was confirmed by the subsequent arrival of the divisions of Ptah and Seth, and the campaign finally ended with a treaty of peace between Ramses II and the Hittite king.

## C. Warfare in the Early Iron Age

Within a half century of the battle of Kadesh, the Iron Age began to dawn in the Near East. Some historians believe that the Hittites of Anatolia were the first people to use iron weapons, and they probably introduced the long-bladed, iron sword to replace the bronze battle axe and the mace. Eventually, iron replaced bronze on spearheads and the heads of arrows. The Philistines, one of several Indo-European "Sea Peoples" (an Egyptian term) who migrated from Greece and the area of the Aegean Sea to the Near East, and perhaps to Italy, coincident to the beginning of the Iron Age, may have acquired their knowledge of iron sword making from the Hittites. In any case, the Philistines overwhelmed the Hittite civilization in Anatolia and their iron swords helped them to cut a wide swath of destruction down the eastern coasts of the Mediterranean through Syria, Lebanon, Canaan, and to the very borders of Egypt. There they met their match in the Egyptian army of Ramses III, one not only equipped with iron swords but also aided by the Sherden, a "Sea People" who had become allies of Egypt.

In fierce fighting on land and sea in 1188 B.C., the Egyptians and the Sherden repelled the invasion of Egypt, and the Philistines eventually settled down to an occupation of coastal Canaan where they established a state called Philistia. (Philistia, in the form of Palestine, eventually became the name of the whole region.) The Philistines established the cities of Askelon, Ashdod, Ekron, Gaza, and Gath on the plain between the mountains of Judah and the Mediterranean, and, at first, they were militarily superior to the other residents of the region. Perhaps less than a century before the Philistines appeared in Palestine, the Israelites—a Hebrew people—had escaped from their bondage in Egypt to the safety of the Sinai desert and then migrated to the desert country east of the river Jordan. Before 1200 B.C. they had crossed the river Jordan, sacked the Canaanite city of Jericho, and established their control over parts of inland Canaan. Then the arrival of the better armed Philistines threatened the Israelites and Canaanites alike, and they were unable to prevent the Philistines from extending their power inland. The Philistines defeated the Israelite army of King Saul decisively at the battle of Mt. Gilboa c. 1050 B.C. and then dominated the Israelites for about a half century.

The Israelites threw off Philistine domination about 1000 B.C., and during the reign of King David they confined Philistine control to the southern coastal region of Palestine. Ancient Israel reached the zenith of its expansion in the reign of King Solomon (965–925 B.C.) when Israel's frontiers encompassed most of Palestine and parts of what are today Lebanon, Jordan, and Syria. Israel also developed good trade relations with the Phoenicians on the coast of Lebanon and probably through them acquired some of their first iron weapons. But even at its zenith Israel was only a local military power, its standing army numbering perhaps 30,000 troops, supported by tribal militia. After Solomon's time, the country was divided into two feuding kingdoms (Israel in the north and Judah in the south), which were vulnerable to invasion by more powerful neighbors.

The new great power in the Near East by the time of Israel's decline was Assyria, on the upper Tigris river. It reached the peak of its powers after 1000 B.C. and possessed its famous capital at Nineveh. Perhaps the most ferocious of all ancient Near Eastern peoples, the Assyrians originally relied on a national militia of perhaps 200,000 men, but King Tiglath-Pileser III eventually formed a standing army of a similar size. The Assyrian kings waged almost continual wars in order to exploit foreign territory for plunder and slaves, and they often marched conquered populations to the Tigris for sacrifice to the Assyrian gods or to exploit their labor.

Besides their ferocity in battle or siege, the Assyrians' military success was due to a thorough exploitation of iron for military purposes and the development of strong shock missile forces properly coordinated on the field of battle. Their expertise in siege craft was unsurpassed to their time. Most of the Assyrian army was composed of battalions of troops armed with spears for shock action, but this sturdy base was powerfully supported by a corps of expert archers, a corps of mobile war chariots, and the first cavalry seen in the Near East in significant numbers. In addition, the Assyrian soldiers were better protected than their enemies by coats of chain-mail armor. With all these military advantages, it is not surprising that Assyria gradually brought most of the Near East under its sway.

In 722 B.C. the Assyrians swept down on Israel and, according to Biblical account, marched away "the ten lost tribes" to oblivion. In 710 B.C., thanks to a plague that broke out in the Assyrian camp, the Judean capital of Jerusalem survived an Assyrian siege, and subsequently the Assyrians weakened their army by impressing too many foreign mercenaries and thereby diluting the army's degree of commitment. When it was faced by increasing foreign resistance and internal rebellions, Assyrian power faltered. The alliance of Neo-Babylonia with Media (in Iran) and other states led to fatal Assyrian defeats. Assyria never recovered from the Neo-Babylonian sacking of its capital at Nineveh in 612 B.C. The collapse of the Assyrian empire left four major states in the Near East: Neo-Babylonia, Media, Egypt, and Lydia in western Anatolia.

### D. War and Persia

Media collapsed before the revolt of the Persians, a subject people living in southwest Iran, and by 550 B.C. Cyrus the Great had created the Kingdom of Medes and Persians. In 547 B.C., the Persians conquered Lydia, and, meanwhile, the kingdom of Judah was caught up in a power struggle between Neo-Babylonia and Egypt. After Babylonia's king Nebuchadnezzar defeated Pharaoh Necho II at the battle of Carchemish in 605 B.C., the Babylonians captured Jerusalem twice, once in 597 B.C. and again in 586 B.C. In the conquest of 586 B.C., the city was destroyed, and many of the surviving Jews were marched away to a "Babylonian Captivity." In turn, the Persians under Cyrus destroyed the Babylonian empire in 539 B.C., and Cyrus freed the Jews and permitted them to reestablish their state in Palestine as a client of the Persians. Though Cyrus died in 530 B.C., his successor Cambyses conquered Egypt in 525 B.C. Thus, only a little more than five hundred years before the birth of Christ, nearly the whole of the Near East was united in one vast Persian empire that stretched over a distance equal to the present width of the continental United States.

Yet, for all of its success in the Near East, Persia's army was not unlike the previous major armies of the region in its essentials, being composed of regular troops supplemented by militia. Counting his bodyguard of 10,000 troops and known as the "Immortals," the Persian king could mobilize as many as three hundred thousand troops by calling on his satraps or territorial governors. Perhaps a third of these were professional soldiers, but many of the troops serving in the Persian army were not Persian. This was especially true of the infantry, which included a great variety of nationalities. And whereas the Persian infantryman was typically armed with a bow or short spear, a dagger or a sword, he was protected only by scale armor and a wicker shield. The Persian cavalryman, armed with bow or javelin, and the similarly armed Persian charioteer, were better protected in chain-mail armor. Though the Persian army's infantry were formidable, its real strength lay in its cavalry and corps of war chariots.

The Persians relied on the Phoenicians to provide them with able sailors and engineers, and, adopting the methods of the Assyrians, they were adept in using the established methods of laying siege to fortified cities and fortresses. They employed the battering ram, the siege tower, the scaling ladder, and the tunnel, but they did not improve on Assyrian techniques by developing the siege catapult (probably invented by the Greek city-state of Syracuse in 399 B.C.). Long before Persia's time, the Mesopotamian peoples had developed all the major technical methods for strengthening brick and stone walls against attack, including the use of bastions, towers, battlements, moats (dry and wet), and sophisticated gates. Again, the Persians were satisfied with the existing means in fortifying key cities in their empire.

## E. Logistics

Logistics—the means by which armies are moved, fed, supplied, and reinforced—was always a critical matter to ancient armies. Ancient soldiers and their porters lived on grain baked into bread or ground into porridge, supplemented by local supplies of meat, fruit, and vegetables. At least twenty pounds of fodder per day per animal had to be provided horses and mules, donkeys a bit less and oxen even more. Because an efficient means of harnessing horses and other draft animals to wagons and carts was lacking (the horse collar and an efficient tandem harness were invented much later by medieval Europe), the loads that could be drawn in such vehicles were much smaller in ancient times than later. In consequence, the armies of the ancient world depended primarily on human backs and pack animals to move supplies overland. A horse, mule, or camel could carry a burden about three times heavier than the load of a human porter, but each kind of animal consumed between five and seven times as much food by weight and at least eight times as much water as a human bearer. The movement of men and supplies by water was the most efficient form of transportation in the ancient world, and, inland, river craft were often used to move supplies for armies on the march. In consequence, the generals of antiquity had to give consideration to capturing sustenance for animals as well as for people, to operating along river lines where possible, and to the conquest of cities as rapidly as possible, lest a well stocked city outlast any attempt to starve it into submission.

## F. Command, Control, and Communications

Command, control, and communications—in modern military jargon often referred to as C to the third power—was at once more simple and more complex in ancient times than today. The means of strategic communications—those for sending messages over long distances and affecting movements before battle—were, of course, primitive compared to today's telephone, radio, and television. In ancient times, they were restricted to such devices such as bonfires, heliographs (using primitive sun reflectors such as shields), and messages carried by couriers in chariots, on horseback, or on foot. Given the uncertainty of weather, the location of the stations, and the limitations on the endurance of men and animals, strategic communication was, by today's standards, slow and not wholly reliable.

Tactical $C^3$—command, control and communication on the actual battlefield—was also primitive by today's standards. The movement of troops was guided by the movement of banners, drum beats, the sound of horns, as well as by voice command. Unless he was taken by surprise, the commander of an army might have the opportunity to arrange his forces before battle to their best advantage relative to the enemy and the terrain, but at best he could directly control only a part of his forces once fighting began. If he remained with his reserve (if there was one) after fighting commenced, he might lose influence with the troops already engaged with the enemy. If he chose to participate in the fighting from the outset he might lose effective control over the forces not in his immediate vicinity. Kings often commanded their armies in person, though a lost battle might deprive a country of its head of state. Most officers were associated with the aristocracy, but all in all we know little about the formal training of the Near Eastern armies, either of the officers or the men.

Staffs of some kind existed from the earliest of times—that is, bodies of men at the commander's headquarters to assist him in personal and professional matters—but staff duties in ancient armies were, as a rule, not specialized. Staff officers often had many and sometimes conflicting duties, and each ancient commander seems to have had his own particular style for collecting intelligence, assigning missions and duties to be performed, and carrying out reconnaissance. The supply and pay functions were doubtless carried out by designated persons, but paperwork was much less than in our own age of typewriters, computers, and word-processors. Probably the commander of an ancient army or a fleet relied on personal briefings of his most important commanders before battle and then trusted his plan (or his doctrine, to use a contemporary term) and the valor of his forces to carry the day. But it is difficult to isolate a "method" of command common to the generals of antiquity; much depended on their innate abilities, the initiative and intelligence of subordinates, their freedom of action (or the lack of it) and, of course, the factors of luck and circumstance.

## G. The Navies

The early navies also played a vital role in the supply, as well as in the transportation, of armies overseas. The Phoenicians and Egyptians were among the first of the Near Eastern peoples to develop relatively efficient warships, transports, and cargo-carriers. The Phoenicians—the great mariners and overseas colonizers of the Near East—largely manned the fleets of Persia, but even the Phoenicians, fine sailors though they were, did not utilize the art of tacking against the wind with large warships. Like all other Mediterranean peoples, they relied primarily on oars rather than sails for propulsion. The galley—with a mast and sail for auxiliary power—was the main means for gaining command of the sea in the Mediterranean throughout the ancient period, but galleys varied greatly by type and capability. Down to 1000 B.C. sea battles were primarily exchanges of arrows and javelins, followed by grappling and boarding, the bronze ram apparently giving only an indifferent performance. Coincident with the coming of the Iron Age, the iron ram was fitted to the bow of the galley in order to puncture an enemy warship below the waterline, but apparently not until about 500 B.C. did the ancient Greeks, especially the Athenians, develop tactics that made the ram effective. Ramming aside, and allowing for the later introduction of the catapult, throughout the ancient period naval battles resembled those ashore except that the fighting occurred across decks rather than over ground.

## III. Early Western Warfare: The Greek Way, 499–362 B.C.

### A. The Military Craft of Hellenic Greece

West of the straits of the Dardanelles, the traditional dividing line between Eastern and Western civilizations until the age of Alexander the Great, a Mycenaean Greek civilization existed during the Bronze Age. We know relatively little about Mycenaean warfare except through tentative archaeological findings and the Homeric poems written hundreds of years after the Trojan War, the legendary conflict about 1200 B.C. between the Greeks and the city of Troy on the Asian side of the straits. As early as 1150 B.C. Mycenaean civilization went into such a decline that it disappeared altogether during the so-called Greek Dark Ages. About 750 B.C. there arose a new and different Hellenic Greek civilization based on the *polis* (city-state), and by 500 B.C. there were about seventy Greek city-states of varying sizes, chief among them Sparta and Athens.

Sparta was the most militaristic of the Greek city-states. The male citizen of Sparta (and only males were citizens) was obliged to place a priority on military preparation over every other activity, and this high state of military readiness was made possible by Spartan exploitation of the *helots,* or slaves, who provided the economic labor of the state. At seven years of age Spartan boys were taken from their mothers to join all other able-bodied Spartan males under thirty years of age for a life in the barracks and military training. Even after his thirtieth birthday, the Spartan male was obligated to take up arms whenever the state was at war. The two kings of Sparta served as the army's commanders in chief. In contrast, Athens had no standing or professional army, but its able-bodied, adult males were required to undergo periodic military training and to serve in the Athenian militia in time of danger. When the militia-army mobilized, the *polemarch* served as its commander in chief and tactical command was rotated on a daily basis among the *strategoi* or generals, one for every *deme* or tribe represented in the army.

Whatever the differences among the various Greek city-state armies, they had in common a reliance on the hoplite, a heavy infantryman who received his appellation from the *hoplon,* his distinctive round shield. His other protection included a helmet with face mask, plate armor for the protection of chest and back, and metal greaves to protect the shins and knees. He was also well armed with a thrusting spear eight to ten feet in length and, for a sidearm, he carried a long-bladed, iron sword. The Greeks relied primarily on shock power to win their battles, the hoplites massing in phalanxes six to eight ranks deep, the spears of the first three ranks leveled at the enemy, the interlocking shields of the phalanx adding to the protection of each hoplite. Though capable of powerful shock action, originally the Greek armies were only weakly supported by cavalry and light infantry armed with missile weapons.

## B. The Persian Wars

In 499 B.C. the Greeks of Ionia—the collective name for the coastal region and adjacent islands of western Asia Minor—rebelled against rulers set over them by the Persians, and Athens and Eritria sent warships to aid the rebellion. The Persians finally crushed the uprising, and, in retribution for the Eritrean and Athenian interference in his affairs, Persian king Darius I dispatched a punitive expedition of 26,000 troops across the Aegean Sea in the summer of 490 B.C. Thus commenced the series of struggles between an Eastern and a Western civilization which have come down to us as the "Persian Wars."

Once across the Aegean Sea, the Persian force in 490 B.C. split into two parts, one going on to lay siege to Eritrea on the island of Euboea and eventually destroying it, the other landing and camping at the bay of Marathon, twenty-six miles north of Athens, until the other Persian force could join it. In response to the danger, Athens dispatched an army of 10,000 troops (including a thousand Plataeans) to the vicinity of the Persian landing. In late September, the Athenians formed their phalanx and launched such a sudden and rapid attack that the Persians scarcely had time to form for battle. With their backs to the sea and with little depth with which to absorb the Greek onslaught, the Persians were unable to exploit their missile weapons in time to prevent the impact of the phalanx from overwhelming them. In consequence, the Persian formation collapsed, and thousands of Persians were slaughtered while fighting on shore or attempting to escape to their ships. The battle of Marathon ended as the first great victory ever enjoyed by a Western army over an Eastern army. Moreover, after learning of the defeat at Marathon and that a Spartan army had arrived to aid the Athenians in defense of their city, the surviving Persian force eventually returned to Asia Minor.

Darius I would have probably dispatched new and more powerful Persian forces against Greece without delay after the humiliating defeat at Marathon had he not been involved in suppressing a revolt in Egypt until his death in 486. But Xerxes, his son and successor, finally put down the revolt in Egypt in 484 and, in the spring of 480, at last set forth against Greece at the head of 200,000 troops, 1,200 warships and 3,000 supply ships and troop carriers. Because the huge Persian army could neither carry with it nor find in Greece enough food and fodder to feed all of its men and animals, Xerxes's strategy hinged on marching his army overland while his fleet operated close off its seaward flank and supplied extra food and fodder. The Persian crossing of the Hellespont near the mouth of the Dardanelles was accomplished by two bridges composed of boats that together constituted a monument to the genius of the Phoenician engineers em-

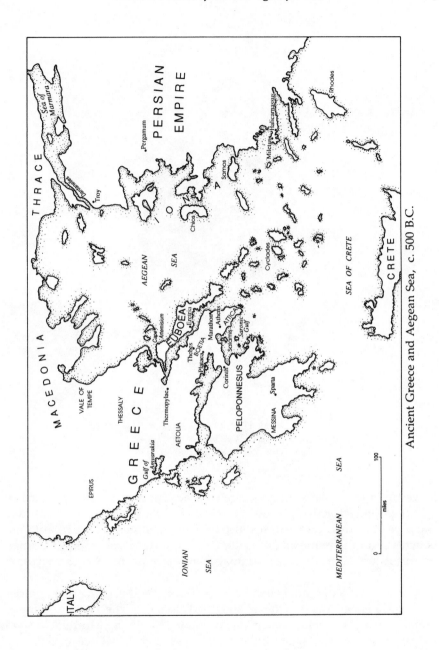

Ancient Greece and Aegean Sea, c. 500 B.C.

Greek Hoplite, c. 480 B.C.
John Warry, *Warfare in the Classical
Age* (New York: St. Martin's, 1980),
p. 35.

ployed by the Persians. One bridge utilized 360 boats, the other 314, all anchored and cabled together in such a way that continuous roadways could be built over them from shore to shore. As the Persian column debouched into the peninsula of Gallipoli on the European shore, it turned north toward Thrace for an eventual march around the Aegean Sea into Greece.

But the Greeks had not been idle since Marathon. Believing that another Persian invasion was inevitable, they had united in the Hellenic League under Sparta's leadership and given attention to building a formidable and mostly Athenian war fleet and fortifying key places in Greece. Still, the Greeks were far outstripped by the Persians in numbers of troops and ships, and, in the crisis of invasion, they made matters worse by their divisiveness over strategy. The city-states of Thessaly wanted the Greek army to make a stand in the vale at Tempe in the north, but the Spartans favored a stand at the isthmus of Corinth in the south. Eventually the Greeks compromised on a stand at the pass of Thermopylae, eighty miles north of Athens. In order to prevent the Persian fleet from landing troops behind this position, the Greek fleet stationed itself off Artemisium at the head of Euboea.

The Greek strategy came close to success. Persian numbers counted for little in the narrow pass at Thermopylae, and for three days in August an army of 7,000 Greeks beat back every Persian assault. But when a Greek deserter informed Xerxes of a poorly defended path around the pass, the "Great King" sent a force by night to rout the small Greek force guarding it. By daybreak the Greek army was threatened with attack on its front and rear. Leonidas, the Spartan king who commanded the Greek army, ordered most of his troops to retreat while he and three hundred fellow Spartans fought to delay the Persians. The delaying action was successful, but Leonidas and his rear guard fell to a man.

News of the Greek army's retreat caused the Greek fleet, which until then had well performed its blocking mission against the Persian fleet, to withdraw down the Euboean channel and around Attica to the Saronic Gulf, where it took up a position in the bay of Eleusis between the western coast of Attica and the island of Salamis, not far from Piraeus, the chief port of Athens. Meanwhile, the Greek army retreated all the way to the isthmus of Corinth, abandoning many places, including the city of Athens, to the oncoming Persians. Xerxes caused his fleet to block all exits from the bay of Eleusis, and in September launched six hundred of his vessels in an attack on the Greek fleet—only half as large—off the island of Salamis.

Few battles in history have had a more surprising outcome than Salamis. The Persian ships in the lead entering the narrow waters proved vulnerable to envelopment and the Greek ships engaged them with ramming tactics, destroying them before the Persian ships in the rear could come to their assistance. This tactic was repeated as a succession of Persian ships tried to enter the bay, and, in a seven-hour battle, the Persians lost two hundred of their ships against a Greek loss of only forty vessels. Xerxes was so shaken by the reverse and the possibility that the Greek fleet would next fall on his vital supply ships that, after detaching 50,000 troops to dispute the Greek recovery of Boeotia and Thessaly and another force to hold Thrace, he led most of his army back to the safety of Asia Minor. Athenian naval power had turned the tide of the war.

Even after the departure of the "Great King" and most of his army from Greece, it was not until July 479 that a mostly Spartan army under the general Pausanias bested the Persians in Boeotia and Thessaly at the battle of Plataea. Another reverse for the Persians was the nearly coeval battle of Mycale on the island of Samsos, hard by the coast of Asia Minor, where a daring Greek expedition caught a beached Persian fleet by surprise, defeated its forces, and burned its vessels. Persian control over Ionia collapsed in the aftermath of the battle, and the Ionians joined the other Greeks in the war against Persia. When the Spartans refused to participate in further operations in Asia Minor, the Athenians in 478 sponsored the Delian

League, a voluntary alliance of Greeks, including the Ionians. The strength of the league was primarily naval. In the same year that the league was formed, the Athenians compelled the surrender of the Persian garrisons holding the Hellespont, and two years later the Persians were obliged to withdraw their garrisons from Thrace.

### C. Athens and the Peloponnesian Wars

By the time Persia made peace with the Greeks in 449 B.C., Athens had established her naval dominance over the Aegean Sea and much of the eastern Mediterranean. But by then it had begun to practice a kind of naval imperialism over the other members of the Delian league that caused many other Greek city-states to look to Sparta to lead in the resistance against Athens. The Greek conflicts gradually intensified until they culminated in the full-blown Peloponnesian Wars (431–404 B.C.). Under the shrewd leadership of Pericles, the early strategy of Athens against its Greek enemies was to seize the offensive at sea while remaining on the defensive on land behind the "Long Walls" leading from Athens to its port of Piraeus. By remaining behind the walls and importing food through Piraeus from traders on the Black Sea, the Athenians could spare themselves the defense of most of Attica and concentrate on amphibious operations against their enemies.

But Athenian strategy over time was partially offset by the rising naval strength of Corinth, Sparta's ally, and, after Pericles's death in 429, the Athenians made a strategic blunder by trying to wage war aggressively on land in Attica. The military and naval demands on Athenian resources were too great and the divided effort only weakened the Athenian position. Matters were made worse in 413 when an Athenian amphibious expedition against Syracuse—a Spartan ally on the island of Sicily in the central Mediterranean—ended in disaster. Thereafter, the Athenian navy was gradually destroyed, much of it while beached at Aegospotami in a daring attack led by the Spartan Lysander in 405. Finally, after the Athenian sea lanes to the Black Sea granaries were cut and the port of Piraeus was blockaded, the Athenian population behind the "Long Walls" was starved into submission in 404 B.C. Under the terms of peace, Athens was forced to destroy the "Long Walls," surrender the remains of her fleet and overseas empire, and recognize Spartan supremacy in Greece.

The civil strife in Greece directly aided Persia in restoring her fortunes in the Aegean region and in the eastern Mediterranean. While the Greeks were preoccupied with fighting each other, the Persians reconquered Ionia and reestablished naval bases in the Aegean Sea. In addition, the excellence of Greek heavy infantry so impressed Persian rulers that hoplites were eagerly sought as mercenaries in the Persian army. Xenophon, a friend of the famous philosopher Socrates, was a mercenary soldier who enlisted under the Spartan general Clearchus to serve Cyrus, satrap of Asia Minor.

Cyrus was planning to oust his brother Artaxerxes II from the throne of Persia, and, after collecting an army of some 30,000 Asian and 13,000 Greek mercenary soldiers, he marched into the heart of the Persian empire in 401 and faced Artaxerxes's army at Cunaxa, sixty miles north of Babylon.

In the battle that followed, the Greek mercenaries were on the point of delivering victory into Cyrus's hands when the Persian leader was killed. His death set off a panic among his Asiatic troops, who fled the battlefield. The unbroken Greeks continued to fight so well that Artaxerxes was content to grant them an armistice and the promise of an undisturbed withdrawal to their homeland. Subsequent Persian treachery caused the Athenian generals to be separated from their men and killed, but the resourceful hoplites elected new generals from among their ranks (Xenophon chief among them) and eventually the "Ten Thousand" marched and fought their way to the safety of the Bosphorus. Xenophon himself provides us with an account of part of this epic campaign in his *Anabasis* ("The Return Up-Country").

In the early fourth century, Sparta's ascendancy in Greece eventually proved as irksome as the earlier Athenian domination, and Greece was again torn by civil war. Thebes took the lead in the revolt against Spartan domination in 378. During the next seven years, Sparta defeated all of the allies of Thebes which was fortunate that, at the Battle of Leuctra in 371, its army was commanded by the talented Epaminondas. Epaminondas achieved a stunning victory over the Spartans by a revision of hoplite tactics. He concentrated his strength on the left wing of his phalanx, where the ranks were increased to fifty deep, and at the head of this column he placed a body of three hundred specially picked shock troops known as the "Sacred Band" and commanded by Pelopidas. When the Spartan army tried to outflank the Theban forces, both Theban cavalry and the heavy column caught the Spartans in motion, and, after a bitter battle, the Spartans were forced to withdraw. The new shock tactics triumphed for the Thebans again at Mantinea in 362, though at the cost of Epaminondas's life. Pelopidas, the only other Theban general in the same class with Epaminondas, had died earlier. After Mantinea, Thebes and Sparta were nearly exhausted and a divided Greece became a tempting target for outside powers.

## IV. The Macedonian Art of War and Alexander the Great

### A. The Macedonian Army

Lying to the north of Greece, but outside Greek civil strife, was the Kingdom of Macedon. The kingdom began to evolve into a major military power after Philip II (the Great) seized the throne in 359 and gained practical experience in warfare in numerous campaigns against Balkan enemies.

Over the course of time he created a formidable army. The Macedonian heavy infantry was armed with the *sarissa*, a spear or pike thirteen feet in length, which allowed the spear points of the first five ranks of the Macedonian phalanx to reach the front instead of the traditional three ranks. The Hypaspists, composing a special force of elite heavy infantry, were quick as well as powerful, and often accompanied cavalry in the attack. The Macedonian light infantry were armed with javelins, slings, and bows, and, as befitted more mobile troops, were protected by less armor than the heavy infantry. The heavy cavalry, the most elite formations of which were known as the King's Companions, were armed with a shorter version of the sarissa, pointed at both ends for convenience of thrusting, while the light cavalry were armed with bows and javelins. Philip also introduced the torsion catapult to the Macedonian army, employing this missile weapon as a species of field artillery as well as a siege weapon. Some of his catapults could hurl a stone weighing sixty pounds as far as 400 yards.

As much as the excellence of its different branches, the tactical effectiveness of the Macedonian army lay in its unprecedented close coordination of arms, even exceeding that of the Assyrians. In general, Philip's method was to use his phalangite heavy infantry to engage their counterparts in the opposing army, using his light infantry and the cavalry to drive their counterparts from the field. Once his cavalry and light infantry had accomplished their missions, they returned to rejoin the Macedonian phalangite infantry in attacking the enemy's heavy infantry with a combination of shock and missile action. The opposing phalanx usually collapsed under the impact of all these attacks. Alexander, Philip's son, would use similar tactics in his conquest of the Persian empire.

Thanks to Philip's reform of Macedonian logistics, the Macedonian army also had unprecedented strategic range. In contrast to other armies, which routinely used all the wagons, carts, and bearers they could muster and placed the burden of moving the army's armor and weapons on the supply train, Philip reserved the use of carts and wagons for the tasks of moving siege equipment, tents, and other exceptionally burdensome materials. He allowed only one pack animal for every fifty soldiers, one porter for every four soldiers, and each soldier was expected to carry his own arms, armor, and personal possessions, and even some of his food and water. Though Philip's measures increased the burden of his soldiers, they also reduced his army's dependence on porters and beasts of burden and permitted his army to make longer strategic marches than would have been possible otherwise. Again, Alexander utilized Philip's logistical system in his conquest of the Persian empire.

Philip's campaigns in Greece eventually gave him control of Thessaly, Thrace, and the straits at the Bosphorus, and in 346 he gained control of the pass at Thermopylae. In 338 his army invaded Boeotia and crushed the Athenian-Theban forces at the battle of Chaeronea, a battle in which Alexander, though only eighteen years old at the time, successfully commanded

Ancient Catapult.
John Warry, *Warfare in the Classical Age* (New York: St. Martin's, 1980),
p. 179.

the right wing of his father's army. Three months after Philip's victory at Chaeronea, a congress of Greek states meeting at Corinth accepted Philip as captain-general of Greece and approved his plans for a Macedonian-Greek army to liberate Ionia from Persian rule. Philip's preparations for war were still underway when he was assassinated in 336. After succeeding his father as king, Alexander III (the Great) reaffirmed Philip's pledge of a war against Persia.

## B. Alexander's Campaigns against Persia

Perhaps 30,000 infantry (7,000 Greeks), 6,000 cavalry, and 16,000 porters and teamsters composed Alexander's army when it crossed the Hellespont in the spring of 334 B.C. As revealed by Alexander's actions, as well as his words, his strategic plan against Persia called for defeating the Persian army in Asia Minor, freeing the Greek cities in Asia, neutralizing the superior Persian fleet (400 Persian warships to 180 Greek warships) by seizing its bases on the periphery of the Mediterranean, and finally striking at the heart of Persian power in Mesopotamia and Iran. His plan extended to the occupation of the interior of Anatolia, which could be exploited for food and fodder, and a psychological aspect of his strategy was his offers of alliance to cities in his path which were willing to desert the Persians. He planned to found Greek cities in the wake of his advance, thereby relieving population pressures in Greece and insuring a nucleus of loyal Greek supporters in areas vacated by his army as it moved deeper into the Persian empire, but it is unclear whether Alexander orginally intended to advance, as he finally did, to the borders of India. From the outset of his expedition, however, his declared goal was to make himself "Lord of Asia."

Persian resistance to Alexander's advance was first organized by the satraps of western Asia Minor with the help of the Greek mercenary general Memnon. Just three days after Alexander's army landed in Asia Minor, a Persian army of 20,000 Greek hoplites and 20,000 Persian cavalry offered battle behind the shallow river Granicus. The Persians deployed their cavalry in a forward line just behind the river, the Greek mercenaries formed in phalanxes on higher ground some distance behind. Upon sizing up the enemy deployment and discovering that the Granicus was fordable, Alexander boldly led an attack on the unsupported cavalry at the the center of the enemy line with a mixed force of Macedonian-Greek cavalry and infantry. As the resistance of the Persian cavalry collapsed, the rest of the Persian mounted forces joined the flight from the battlefield. Memnon's mercenary hoplites in the rear were left alone to contend against Alexander's army, and the subsequent carnage was so great that only 2,000 of the Greek mercenaries were taken alive. Reputedly, Alexander's losses for the whole battle came to 150 men.

In Alexander's further advance, his army's capture of the naval bases at Miletus and Halicarnarsus forced the Persian fleet to retreat further east, and, after his army had exploited the food and fodder in Anatolia, he led it through Cilicia and started down the coast of Syria. Then he learned that Darius III and a Persian army of 80,000 infantry and 20,000 cavalry and charioteers were marching across his rear. Promptly, he countermarched in order to deal with this threat to his communications and in November 333 B.C. encountered Darius's army behind the river Pinarus and next to the Gulf of Issus. Again the stream in front of the Persian position was fordable, though the opposing banks were high and in places fortified.

Rather than endure the rain of Persian missiles as his forces approached the river bank, Alexander put himself at the head of his troops and led an attack on the left center of Darius's line. As the Persian line collapsed at this point, the Alexandrian cavalry passed through the gap, Darius fled from the field, and Alexander's right wing wheeled to drive the Persians against their own fortifications. Tens of thousands of them were killed during the battle or in the pursuit that followed.

Though Alexander must have been sorely tempted in the wake of his victory at Issus to advance directly into Mesopotamia, he returned to his original strategy of seizing the Mediterranean bases of the Persian fleet before advancing deeper into the Persian empire. This strategy encountered a major stumbling block when his army reached Tyre. Built on an island half a mile from the mainland, the city was completely enclosed by walls up to one hundred fifty feet in height. In January 332 B.C., Alexander put his men and the local population to building a mole as a bridge to Tyre, a tremendous filling project that required six months to construct. Com-

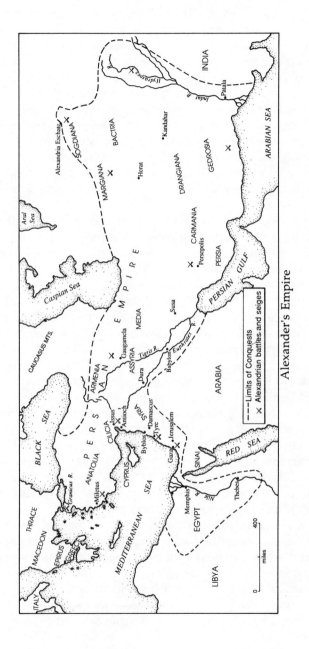

Alexander's Empire

pleted, it was two hundred feet broad and in places twenty feet deep. While the work was underway, Darius sent word that he was willing to concede the western part of his empire to Alexander if he would make peace. Alexander spurned the offer and the siege continued. When the mole placed Tyre within range of his catapults, Alexander had two siege towers built to house them, each tower fifteen stories high. When the enemy burned down the towers in a raid, he had them rebuilt. Seven months after the siege began, Alexander's army breached Tyre's defenses and the city surrendered. During the siege, his army had lived on the supplies levied on neighboring cities which had not resisted his advance. The conquest of Tyre was a major accomplishment, in some ways more difficult even than Alexander's defeat of the Persian armies at the Granicus and at Issus.

After capturing Tyre, Alexander resumed his march, overcoming resistance at Gaza and entering Egypt in November 332. Welcomed by the Egyptians as the new god-king, Alexander rested his army over the winter, and then, in the spring of 331 B.C., led 47,000 troops north toward Mesopotamia. His army reached the upper waters of the Euphrates in August, whereupon it learned that Darius had caused all local food and fodder down the entire length of the river to be withdrawn to fortified cities. Alexander defeated Darius's strategy by leading his army to the upper valley of the Tigris where food and fodder supplies were still readily accessible, and, as his army advanced down the Tigris, Darius led an army of perhaps 150,000 men to intercept it on the plain of Gaugamela. The subsequent battle on October 1 was the largest in Alexander's career.

Facing a host that outnumbered his army several times, Alexander's chief hope lay in striking the enemy line near its center where the banners of the Immortals suggested Darius was located and before the wings of the Persian army could engulf his own. But Darius seized the initiative by commencing the Battle of Gaugamela (Arbela) by unleashing a chariot and cavalry assault against the left of Alexander's line. The fury of the attack bent the line back into a refused flank, and some of the Persian cavalry even rode on to raid the Macedonian-Greek camp several miles away. But Alexander's heavy infantry finally absorbed the onslaught of the Persian chariots, and when a large part of the Persian army then advanced to the aid of the charioteers, it left the gap in the Persian line that Alexander was seeking. Alexander personally led his remaining forces into the gap and toward Darius's location, and, as the Macedonian infantry broke through the center of the Persian line, Darius fled the field. Instead of pursuing the fleeing Persian king, Alexander swung the "hammer" of his right wing against an enemy caught between it and the "anvil" formed by his left, and the rest of the Persian army was defeated. By day's end perhaps 40,000 Persians lay dead or dying on the field. Alexander's losses are believed to have amounted to only a few hundred men.

Darius III lost more than a battle and an army at Gaugamela; his prestige was so shattered by the defeat that the next year, while he was in his retreat near the Caspian Sea, he was slain by his own nobles. Prince Bessus assumed his mantle. In the meantime, Alexander encountered little further resistance in his conquest of Mesopotamia and western Iran, and, after the fall of the Persian capital at Persepolis, captured in January 330, Alexander allowed many of his Greek soldiers to return home. He reorganized the remainder of his army to pursue Bessus, who had withdrawn further east.

Alexander's subsequent campaigns in the far-off lands of Parthia, Margiana, Sogdiana, and Bactria—now comprising parts of Iran, Afghanistan, and Soviet Central Asia—were some of the most difficult of his career, and between 329 and 327 B.C. he and his army were engaged in almost constant combat, sometimes with elusive mountain tribesmen who waged a formidable guerrilla war. But Alexander fashioned lightly equipped, fast-moving forces to deal with such enemies, and gradually beat the tribesmen at their own game. He also founded a number of Greek cities, and, in consequence, Hellenic and Asian cultures began to meld into a common Hellenistic civilization. In 327 Alexander's army left Afghanistan and entered the territory of King Porus in what is now Pakistan with 15,000 infantry and 5,000 cavalry. To oppose Alexander's invasion, Porus raised an army of 30,000 infantry, 4,000 cavalry, three hundred chariots and two hundred war elephants. Alexander was able to defeat Porus only with difficulty at the Battle of the Hydaspes river in 326, and he was so impressed with him in an interview after the battle that, following Porus's oath of fealty, he restored him to his throne.

Alexander perhaps contemplated a campaign to make himself master of India, but he finally marched his army down the river Indus to the Indian Ocean, then returned it to Mesopotamia, some of the men marching overland and others returning on a fleet built for that purpose. Back in Mesopotamia, Alexander chose Babylon to be the capital of his empire, but he had hardly taken up residence there when, in June 323 B.C., he took sick and died short of his thirty-third birthday. His principal generals divided his domains among themselves. The final legacies of Alexander's conquests were three Alexandrian "successor empires"—the Antigonid, the Seleucid, and the Ptolemaic, a Hellenistic culture in the eastern Mediterranean and the Near East, and an imperishable tradition of the hero-warrior-king.

## V. Ancient Warfare in India and China

Little is known about Indian civilization before 2000 B.C., when an Aryan people closely related to the Persians crossed the Hindu Kush and invaded India from the northwest. The dark-skinned population already living in India were conquered or driven into the extreme south, but an amalgamation of races and cultures apparently took place, producing the Hindu civilization. The Aryan Hindus made themselves masters of the Indus and Ganges river valleys especially, but down to c. 600 B.C. our knowledge of the Indian military is derived from the classical Indian literature, especially the *Rigveda* and the *Mahabharata*. These sources suggest that the Indian armies were composed almost entirely of infantry armed with bow and javelin, there were few horses, and the relatively few chariots were reserved for kings and commanders. In contrast with the armies of the Near East, those of India did not commonly possess iron weapons before c. 500 B.C., nor did they take much interest in heavy infantry of the phalangite variety. Close fighting was not highly organized and often degenerated into a melee. Near Eastern influences may have been at work in India by the time of Alexander the Great, for the army of King Porus had a military organization more like the Persian.

Chinese civilization first appeared along the Yellow river about 1600 B.C., and, under the Shang dynasty, it had spread over much of northern China by 1027 B.C. Then a semi-barbarian people called the Chou overwhelmed the Shang empire, extended their rule over most of China, and efficiently organized it under a centralized monarchy. Until nearly 1000 B.C., the Chinese art of war kept pace with that of the Near East, but the Chinese armies were slower than the Near Eastern in embracing iron weapons and chain-mail armor. Their armies probably did not compare in effectiveness with that of Assyria of the same period, though their strong suit was the bow. Bronze weapons, which had appeared in the era of the Shang dynasty, remained the Chinese mainstay down to 600 B.C., long after they were abandoned for iron weapons in the Near East and southeastern Europe. The Chinese employed war chariots at least as early as 1400 B.C., and, as happened in the Near East, they were an important form of mounted warfare in China long before cavalry appeared.

Ancient China can claim to have produced the oldest surviving treatise on warfare, Sun Tzu's *Art of War*, composed c. 500 B.C. Sun Tzu served the maritime state of Wu at the mouth of the Yangtze river and apparently was its preeminent general. In his treatise, Sun Tzu was not primarily interested in the elaboration of involved strategems, nor was he interested in the superficial and transitory techniques of warfare. Rather, his treatise sought to provide a practical guide for the successful prosecution of war based on social, economic, geographical, and psychological factors. Regarding war in distant places, he writes in a manner that Alexander the Great would have understood. According to Sun Tzu, those adept at war do not require a second levy of conscripts, nor more than one provisioning, for invading distand parts. The army should carry equipment from the homeland, but it should rely on the resources of the enemy for its provisions. When one's own country is impoverished by military operations, Sun Tzu wrote, it is usually due to the attempt to meet distant needs from home resources. Hence, the wise general sees to it that his troops feed on the enemy. As Sun Tzu expressed it, one bushel of the enemy's provisions is worth a hundred bushels carried from afar, one hundredweight of the enemy's fodder is worth twenty hundredweight brought from the home country.

# TWO

# War in the Age of Rome

## I. The Roman Army, 509–146 B.C.

### A. The Early Roman Army

About the time the career of Alexander the Great was coming to its end, a new military power in the West—the Roman republic—was beginning its ascent. Less than two hundred years earlier, Rome had been merely one of several Latin-speaking cities in west-central Italy under the domination of the Etruscans. When Rome threw off Etruscan domination in 509 B.C. to become an independent republic, it was ruled by a Senate (a council of elders) drawn from the wealthy patrician class, possessed a land area of about fifty square miles, and its militia-army was similar to those of the Greek city-states of the period.

Originally, the term *legio* (legion) meant a draft or levy of heavy infantry drawn from the property-owning citizen-farmers living around Rome. In Rome's earliest days of independence there were only three legions, each of a thousand men, supplemented by light infantry provided by the poorer citizens and cavalry by the wealthy patrician class. Tribunes of the equestrian or petty noble class commanded the legions, and centurions, promoted or elected from the ranks, commanded the ten centuries into which each legion was divided. After 362 B.C., *imperium*, or the authority to command the Roman army, was entrusted to the consuls, the two chief magistrates of the Roman state, or to their junior colleagues, the praetors.

The Roman army was similar to the Greek of the period, and the earliest Roman Tactics emphasized the phalanx, each legionnaire being armed with a long spear or pike, and a long-bladed sword of the Greek style. He was protected by a bronze-and-leather helmet, chest and back armor, greaves for the shins, and a *scrutum* (an oblong, iron-reinforced wood and leather shield). By 350 B.C., with a growth in the Roman population, the number of Roman legions had been expanded to four, and the number of legionnaires per legion had grown to 3,600. By this time the centuries had been reduced from a hundred men to sixty men apiece, and the sixty centuries in each legion were divided among ten cohorts for administrative purposes. Also by this time Rome had reduced some of the Italian cities in its vicinity to subordination, granting to some varying degrees of citizenship and to others the status of dependent allies. The allied cities were required to provide cavalry and light infantry support to the legions, but men could only serve in the legions if they met citizenship and property-owning requirements. Still, the Roman military forms were essentially Greek, and, until the late fourth century B.C., the Romans had made no distinctive mark on the patterns of war.

## B. The Maniple Legion

The great change in Roman military organization occurred during the Samnite Wars (326–304 B.C.) in central Italy when the Roman legion abandoned Greek methods, partially reequipped its heavy infantry, and adopted new tactics. The new legion, like the old, was divided for administrative purposes into ten cohorts, but the strength of its heavy infantry was raised to 4,200 men, and—counting assigned cavalry, engineers, and staff—its total strength was about 6,000 men. The most striking aspects of the new organization were that the legionnaires were designated respectively as *hastati* (first line), *principes* (second line), and *triarii* (third line) according to their assignment on the battlefield, and only the centuries of triarii retained the long spear traditionally associated with heavy infantry. Each soldier of the hastati and principes was rearmed with two javelins (one light for longer-distance throwing and one heavier for short-range hurls), and with a sword with a blade about two feet in length, known as the *gladius*. In effect, the hastati and principes were combination missile-shock infantrymen. For tactical purposes, every two centuries of them were combined into *manipuli* (maniples or "handfuls") of 120 men apiece.

The tactical deployment of the maniple legion on the battlefield was almost revolutionary when compared with those of phalangite armies of the past. While screened from the enemy on their front by the *velites* (light infantry), and with their flanks protected by cavalry, the hastati, principes, and triarii formed their respective lines, each line separated from the next line by intervals of about thirty yards, and the maniples in the same line separated from each other by intervals equal to about the width of a maniple. Each maniple of the hastati and principes usually formed six ranks deep and twenty files across, and the centuries of the triarii (only sixty men apiece) in six ranks and ten files across. The typical frontage of a deployed legion was 200–250 yards, and the whole formation presented a checkerboard appearance.

If the enemy attacked first, the screen of Roman light infantry delayed his advance long enough for the hastati to fall back into the intervals of the principes of the second line and thus to offer a continuous and reinforced front to the enemy. If the Romans seized the initiative, the light infantry would withdraw, the maniples of principes would advance into the intervals between those of the hastati, and the reinforced line would advance to hurl its javelins and then close for action with its swords. In both situations, the triarii functioned as a reserve. The men in the rear ranks of the hastati and principes periodically relieved those at the front or replaced the fallen, and thus the new organization added endurance to the other advantages of flexibility, combined missile-shock action and the ability to fight on offense or defense.

The maniple legion was superior to any military organization created to its time, and it probably played a decisive role in the Roman defeat of an army of Samnites, Etruscans, and Gauls at the Battle of Sentium in 295 B.C., the last organized opposition to the Romans in central Italy. The Romans then focused their expansion on the southern part of the Italian peninsula, an area heavily colonized by the Greeks. The maniple legion was put to another test when, in order to contain the Roman expansion, Tarentum (Taranto), a Greek city-state on the "heel" of the Italian "boot," forged an alliance with King Pyrrhus of Epirus (roughly present-day Albania), who led an army to its rescue. The struggle against Pyrrhus proved to be a difficult one, and over its course the Roman army experienced two major defeats. The fault did not, however, lie in the maniple legion, but in the Roman consular and praetorian system of command which did not always produce good generals. Moreover, even when Pyrrhus's army was victorious over the Romans it suffered severe casualties; the term "pyrrhic victory" (a hollow triumph) dates back to Pyrrhus's costly victory at Heraclea in 280 B.C. The Romans finally defeated Pyrrhus's army decisively at Beneventum in 275 B.C., and by 265 B.C. Tarentum and the other Greek cities in southern Italy had accepted the status of Roman allies.

### C. The First Punic War

The most formidable opponent ever faced by the Roman republic in the Mediterranean basin was Carthage (also known as Punis), a former Phoenician colony on the coast of North Africa, which over time had evolved into a formidable military and naval power. By the time Rome had conquered southern Italy, Carthage controlled much of North Africa, islands in the western Mediterranean, and much of the Iberian peninsula (Spain and Portugal). The First Punic War (264–241 B.C.) broke out as the result of Roman-Carthaginian rivalry in the island of Sicily.

The Romans learned early in that conflict that lack of naval power could put them at a great disadvantage. The Carthaginian galley fleet could threaten the sea communications of the Roman armies in Sicily and at the same time reinforce and resupply the Carthaginian armies. The Romans first tried to close the gap at sea by building warships modeled on the Carthaginian triremes (fast, agile galleys propelled by three staggered banks of oars, and designed for maneuver and ramming), but in such vessels the Roman advantage in infantry could not be fully exploited. The Romans soon turned to building the quinquereme, a larger ship than the trireme and essentially a troop carrier propelled by a single bank of oars. Though slower and less maneuverable than the trireme, the quinquereme

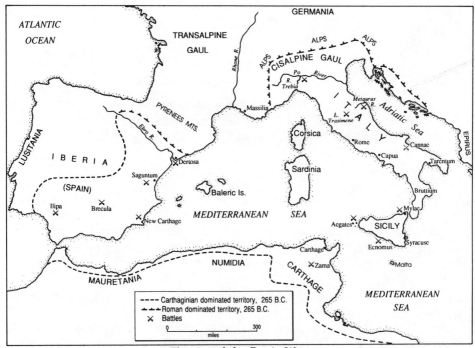

Theater of the Punic Wars

carried a complement of 120 fighting men and was well suited for grappling and boarding.

In order to insure that the Carthaginian vessels could be boarded, the Romans adopted a Syracusan invention called the *corvus* or "crow," an eighteen-foot-long gangway with a pointed iron spike under its outboard end. Pivoted from a mast by a topping lift, the corvus could be dropped with such force on the deck of an enemy warship that its spike would secure itself firmly in the planking; once in place, the corvus offered a bridge across which the Roman infantry could invade the enemy ship and bring its crew to hand-to-hand combat. The corvus proved itself in 260 B.C. when Consul Gaius Duilius took 120 Roman and allied vessels to sea and, in the battle of Mylae off the northern coast of Sicily, inflicted a heavy defeat on the Carthaginian fleet. The corvus also helped the Romans to win a second naval victory in a battle near Cape Ecnomus on the southern coast of Sicily.

Still, the Romans did not easily conclude the First Punic War. Storms at sea caused the loss of two Roman fleets, and the Carthaginian navy further redressed the naval balance with a victory at Drapana in 250 B.C. But persistence, a key Roman virtue, finally paid off, and in 242 a Roman fleet dealt such a decisive defeat to the Carthaginian navy in the battle of the Aegates islands near the western tip of Sicily that Carthage sued for peace the following year. Under the peace terms, Carthage left Sicily in the Roman

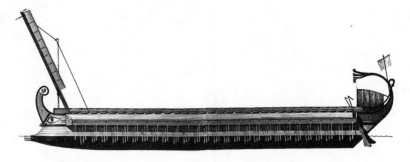

Roman Quinquereme with Corvus.
John Warry, *Warfare in the Classical Age* (New York: St. Martin's, 1980),
p. 118.

sphere and paid the republic a war indemnity. The price of victory for the Roman federation, then with a population of perhaps 3.75 million, was high: 200,000 casualties and the loss of five hundred ships.

### D. The Second and Third Punic Wars

The Second Punic War (219–201 B.C.) had its origins in Carthaginian-Roman rivalries in the Iberian peninsula, war breaking out in 219 B.C. over the status of the city of Saguntum. After defeating the Roman forces in Iberia in 218, Hannibal Barca, the Carthaginian commander-in-chief in Spain, led an army of 40,000 troops and thirty-seven war elephants on an epic march across southern Gaul (France), the Alps, and into Cisalpine Gaul (a part of northern Italy). Despite a heavy attrition of his forces from the long march, in December 218 B.C. Hannibal lured a Roman army into making a rash winter attack on his army over the river Trebia and inflicted a heavy defeat on the Romans in the northern Italian plains. After resting his army in northern Italy over the winter and adding 10,000 Gallic warriors to its ranks, Hannibal marched on Rome in the spring of 217.

Once again a Roman army acted imprudently and, in its eagerness to get at the Carthaginians, marched into Hannibal's trap set on the banks of Lake Trasimene in April. As its surviving remnants fled, the other army seemed unlikely to take Hannibal's measure; in the crisis, Quintus Fabius Maximus was elected Roman dictator and granted emergency powers. But he was soon dubbed "Cunctator," or "Delayer," for he refused to risk a general battle in the field with Hannibal. Instead, he relied on Rome's fortifications to fend off a direct attack and the tactics of harassment (since called fabian tactics) with the remaining Roman army in the field to hinder Carthaginian foraging. Since Hannibal had no siege train, and his army had to keep moving in order not to exhaust local food and forage, Fabius's strategy worked within limits. Near the end of the summer of 217, Hannibal abandoned his operations near Rome, led his army across the Apennines to the eastern side of the Italian peninsula, and ravaged southeastern Italy.

Fabius's strategy seemed to be no answer to Hannibal's new threat, and in 216 B.C. consuls Lucius Aemilius Paullus and Gaius Terentius Varro set out with an army of 80,000 troops to track down Hannibal's force. In August, the Roman army caught up with the Carthaginians near the village of Cannae (modern Barletta) in Apulia. Hannibal caused his army—outnumbered at least two to one—to form a long line of troops with a weak center but strong wings. Since it was Varro's day to command on the Roman side, he led his army into Hannibal's trap by concentrating the Roman attack on the weak Carthaginian center. As the center slowly yielded under pressure, Hannibal's cavalry routed the Roman cavalry and then joined the two wings of Hannibal's army to envelop the Roman flanks. The outcome was encirclement of Varro's command and the worst defeat ever suffered by an army of the Roman republic. Though Varro and 10,000 of his men managed to escape death or capture, Paullus was among the 60,000 Roman soldiers killed. Perhaps 10,000 Romans were taken prisoner.

The defeat at Cannae and subsequent Roman defeats sorely tried the Roman federation, and that it survived so many setbacks and losses is a testament to its resources, determination, and the loyalty of most of its members. But its survival was also due to the ineffectiveness of Hannibal's measures against strongly fortified cities and the inability of his army to remain in any locality for very long. The cities loyal to Rome served as islands of refuge for Roman armies between disasters, and there was sufficient food and implements of war in them that the Romans could always resume the struggle. Moreover, Hannibal eventually required reinforcements, and when his brother Hasdrubal responded by leading troops across the Alps into northern Italy in 207 B.C., his army was intercepted by a Roman army and annihilated at the Battle of the Metaurus river. The defeat was probably the turning point of the war, for when news of Hasdrubal's defeat and death reached southern Italy, many of Hannibal's allies deserted him. He was finally forced to withdraw his dwindling army into Bruttium in the "forestep" and "toe" of the Italian "boot."

Matters worsened for Carthage when, in 206 B.C., Publius Cornelius Scipio the Younger—son of a general by the same name whom Hannibal had defeated at the Trebia and who later died fighting in Iberia—defeated the Carthaginians in Spain. In 204 Scipio led an invasion of North Africa, and in 203 Hannibal returned from Italy with 12,000 troops in order to assemble forces for the defense of Carthage. His army and Scipio's finally met in a decisive battle at Zama in 202, each side having about 40,000 men. But the Roman side was of better quality, and Scipio proved to be in the same class of general as Hannibal. At the outset of the Battle of Zama, Hannibal launched his elephants at the Roman front line, but Scipio's well-drilled maniples quickly formed pathways that encouraged the beasts to bypass them and then struck them in the flank with their javelins. Meanwhile, Scipio's cavalry (Italian and Numidian) launched a counterattack that routed the Carthaginian mounted army and enveloped the flanks of Hannibal's infantry. Scipio's infantry then smashed their way through three lines of opposing Carthaginian troops, the third being destroyed in conjunction with a cavalry attack on its rear, a fitting revenge for Cannae. Though Hannibal avoided death or capture at Zama, perhaps 20,000 Carthaginians died on the field and, as a consequence, Carthage was forced to sue for peace the following year.

Carthage was never again a major power after the Second Punic War, though Roman fears of a Carthaginian revival helped to set off a Third Punic War (149–146 B.C.) that led to the razing of Carthage and the division of its North African territory between Numidia and the Roman province of "Africa." But the greatest military heroes to emerge from the Punic Wars were Scipio (dubbed Africanus) and Hannibal. The latter's reputation remained high even after the Second Punic War, and he found military appointments under various eastern rulers, dying by his own hand in 183 B.C. only in order to avoid being betrayed into the hands of the Romans. Not even the Roman army, the best in the Mediterranean world in Hannibal's day, had made much headway against him until a general of Scipio's talents supplied the want in Roman leadership.

## II. Roman Expansion, Reforms, and Civil Wars to 29 B.C.

### A. Roman Expansion and the Cohort Legion

Rome's potential enemies in the east were states which had evolved from the "successor empires" of Alexander the Great. The three major powers were Macedon, Syria, and Egypt, and the five lesser states were Pergamum, Bithynia, Cappadocia, Pontus, and Galatia. The ambitions of the Macedonian and Syrian kings posed a special threat to Roman security in the eastern Mediterranean, and, somewhat against their will, the Romans were repeatedly involved in wars in the region. The last great stand of the traditional phalangite army against the Romans occurred at the Battle of Pydna in 168 B.C., and in that battle, despite being outnumbered, a Roman army inflicted a crushing defeat on the Macedonian-Greek army of King Perseus. By 130 B.C. Rome had established its dominion over Greece, Macedonia, and much of Asia Minor. In the west, Rome had conquered southern Gaul (southern France) and most of North Africa before 100 B.C.

About a century before the birth of Christ, a number of changes in the Roman army occurred that had great military, social, and political implications, and some of which are associated with the consulship of Gaius Marius. On the military side, one of the Marian reforms involved the conversion of the cohort from an administrative to a tactical unit by making uniform the arms and equipment of the legion's heavy infantry—all of whom were equipped with the javelin and short sword—and by raising the number of legionnaires in each legion to 4,800 men. On the battlefield, every three maniples of 160 men each were combined into a tactical cohort of 480 men formed in six ranks and eighty files. The three lines of cohorts were arranged in the traditional checkerboard pattern. Counting its usual allotment of auxiliary troops, each legion still numbered about 6,000 men.

Marius also tried to improve the mobility of the Roman army by allowing only one pack animal for every fifty men, hence the infantryman carried his own arms, armor, entrenching tools, personal possessions, and some of his food and drink on the march. (The Roman infantrymen referred to themselves jokingly as "Marius's mules.") Though his load might be as much as eighty or ninety pounds, the Marian infantryman was capable of covering up to twenty miles a day over good roads and then helping to fortify the army's camp as a precaution against nocturnal attack, a standard Roman practice when in hostile country. By the time of the cohort legion, the ordinary soldier could look forward to promotion through the various grades of centurion, which by this time represented a whole class of officers. The senior centurion of a legion had considerable status, and the five senior centurions of each legion were included in councils of war held by commanders of field armies. The tribunes, six to a legion, were increasingly young equestrians passing through their apprenticeship in command.

Marius also dropped the property-owning qualification for service in the legion and entrusted the duties of light infantry and cavalry to *auxilia* (auxiliaries) of non-citizen and non-Italian mercenaries serving in separate cohorts of infantry or *alae* (regiments) of cavalry. The source of soldiers for the legions was further increased after 88 B.C., when nearly all Italian freemen were granted Roman citizenship, but by then the importation of slave labor and the consolidation of small farms into vast *latifundia* (plantations) were eroding the class of yeoman farmers which had always been the backbone of the Roman army. Displaced rural Romans were moving in large numbers to the cities, especially to Rome, where they subsisted on whatever work they could get and handouts from the state. There they were call *proletarii* because their critics claimed they raised nothing but *proles* or children.

The proletariat became a natural recruiting source for soldiers under the circumstances, but reliance on them had profound political effects on the Roman army. Instead of meeting their military obligation and returning home, as most of the rural-based soldiers had done, many of the proletariat opted for the life of the professional soldier. The day had begun to wane when a Roman soldier was a citizen first and a soldier second. Such was the character of the Roman army with which Gaius Julius Caesar conquered Gaul in the last major expansion under the Roman republic between 58 and 50 B.C. As proconsul (governor with *imperium*) of Cisalpine and Transalpine Gaul, Caesar had at his disposal at various times between six and

Roman Legionnaire.
John Warry, *Warfare in the Classical
Age* (New York: St. Martin's, 1980),
p. 186.

eleven legions, and, counting auxiliaries, the strength of his army varied
between 40,000 and 70,000 men. Through many long and difficult campaigns and many shared hardships, it is not surprising that Caesar's soldiers came to identify more with him than with the Roman state.

Caesar's military reputation was mostly made in wars against the Gauls,
peoples who actually called themselves Celts, spoke related languages, and
inhabited the areas of western Europe corresponding to modern Britain,
France, Belgium, southern Holland, Switzerland, and Germany west of the
Rhine. Most Gauls were semi-barbarian (influenced to a degree by Roman
culture), but remained organized into tribes, and—armed with javelin,
spear and sword—were noted for their fierce fighting spirit. Across the
Rhine the even fiercer Germanic tribes were often a threat to Roman Gaul,
and, in his Gallic commentaries, Caesar tells us of a battle in 58 B.C. in
which perhaps 40,000 Roman soldiers faced an invasion of Gaul by perhaps
150,000 of the Germanic Helvetii and their allies the Boii and Tulingi.

According to Caesar's account, on the day of this unnamed battle, he sent his cavalry to delay the enemy's approach and withdrew the rest of his troops to a nearby hill. He drew up the four veteran legions in his army in three lines of six ranks each halfway up the hill, and gave orders that the two legions recently levied in northern Italy, and all the auxiliary troops save cavalry, should be posted on the summit. The summit was quickly converted into an earthwork fortification (as a result of the Marian reforms, all Roman soldiers carried spades and stakes as part of their equipment), and the packs and baggage were collected there. Caesar also ordered that the officers' horses, including his own, should be taken to the summit so that no one could entertain the notion that safety could be attained through flight.

The Helvetii were the first to arrive before the Roman position. Without waiting for their allies to appear, they formed a huge mass of warriors and launched an assault on the slope on which the Roman army was posted. The Romans had the advantage because of their elevation, and their rain of javelins stopped the enemy advance in its tracks. Then the soldiers of the veteran legions drew their swords and advanced to engage the enemy in hand-to-hand fighting. Though the Helvetii stoutly resisted, they were finally forced to begin a slow withdrawal toward a hill about a mile away, the four veteran legions following.

The Helvetii had just gained the safety of the hill when Caesar was faced with a crisis. Crowds of Boii and Tulingi appeared on the right flank of the advancing Roman legions and threatened their rear. Seeing this development, the Helvetii began to press forward once more to renew the battle. But Roman drill and discipline saved the day. In order to cope with the situation, Caesar caused his Romans to form a double-front, the first and second lines to oppose the Helvetii, and the third line to form a new front at an angle to the first to hold out against the newly arrived enemy. The battle, fiercely fought, continued in two directions from early afternoon until evening, and Caesar records that not a single Gaul was seen to run away. But finally, after they had suffered perhaps 20,000 casualties, the Helvetii and their allies gave way before the Roman advance, abandoned their camp and baggage, and took flight under the cover of darkness. Though Caesar gives us no figures on Roman casualties in this battle, apparently the Roman army, though victorious, had suffered heavily too. Caesar records that it remained on the battlefield three days in order to bury its dead, treat its wounded, and rest before commencing a pursuit.

### B. The Civil Wars

As mentioned above, the professionalization of the Roman armies led their soldiers to identify with particular commanders, and by 53 B.C. the three leading Roman generals were Caesar, Cnaeus Pompeius Magnus (Pompey) and Marcus Licinius Crassus. The balance of power among this triumvirate was upset that year when Crassus was killed in the defeat of his army at the hands of the Parthians at the Battle of Carrhae in Meso-potamia. After Crassus's death, Pompey secured election by the Senate as sole consul and intrigued to have Caesar relieved of his proconsulship in Gaul. When the Senate ordered Caesar to lay down his command in January 49 B.C., he reacted by leading his legions across the river Rubicon (the southern boundary of his province in northern Italy) and marching on the capital. His action triggered the first of a series of civil wars that would wrack the Roman empire for the next twenty years.

Pompey fled to the east where the Roman legions rallied to him, and, after suppressing resistance in Italy and Spain, Caesar decisively defeated Pompey's forces at the Battle of Pharsalus in Greece in 48 B.C. When, in the wake of his defeat, Pompey fled to Egypt, Caesar's army followed, but arrived only to find that the Egyptian king had caused Pompey to be killed. Caesar placed Cleopatra, the king's sister, on the throne and put Egypt under Roman protection. After restoring order to the rest of the empire, Caesar ruled at Rome with dictatorial powers until March 44 B.C., when a disaffected group in the Senate brought about his assassination.

A further discussion of the Roman civil wars is unnecessary except to mention two battles of particular interest, both naval. The Battle of Nauch-olus was fought off the northeast coast of Sicily between a fleet loyal to Gaius Octavius (Octavian, Caesar's grandnephew, adopted son and heir) and one commanded by Sextus Pompey, son of Pompey the Great, in September 36 B.C. Each fleet consisted of two hundred galleys, but the fleet supporting Octavian, commanded by Marcus Vipsanius Agrippa, harbored a secret weapon, the *harpago,* which consisted of a heavy timber with an iron claw at one end and a long line attached to the other. Fired from a catapult aboard ship, it hooked an enemy vessel and enabled Agrippa's men to haul it close aboard for boarding. Pompey, who had counted on outmaneuvering and ramming his opponents with his faster, more agile galleys, was taken by surprise by Agrippa's weapon, and only seventeen of his two hundred ships survived the battle. Agrippa lost only three ships.

The second battle of interest was that of Actium off the coast of Greece in 31 B.C., which was the last great naval battle in the Mediterranean basin for centuries to come. By then the opposition to Octavian was led by Marc Antony and Cleopatra, queen of Egypt, and Antony's wife since 37 B.C. While Octavian's and Antony's armies faced each other in fortified camps ashore, Agrippa's and Antony's fleets clashed near the entrance of the Gulf of Amvrakia (or Ambracia). Agrippa's 260 galleys surprised the 200 vessels under Antony by using catapults to hurl pots of flaming charcoal into their vessels. The confusion engendered by Agrippa's tactics enabled his vessels to penetrate the enemy's formation and to ram or board. As the battle turned against Antony, his reserve force of galleys under Cleopatra pushed through the confused fighting and set off for Egypt. Antony also managed to flee to Egypt in a galley, but what was left of his fleet withdrew into the Gulf of Amvrakia. A week later both Antony's army and fleet surrendered to Octavian. Octavian's forces subsequently invaded Egypt, and in 30 B.C. Antony and Cleopatra committed suicide. Octavian returned to Rome in 29 B.C., and by then he enjoyed such authority that he was largely free to reshape the government and army to his liking.

## III. The Army of Imperial Rome

### A. From Caesar Augustus to Domitian

Octavian understood that nothing had contributed more directly to the failure of the republic than the growth of client armies and the inability of the Senate to control their commanders, and he was determined that the same fate would not befall his regime. He set about designing a system under which the army would be clearly subordinate to him, choosing the title of *princeps civium Romanorum* ("First of Roman Citizens"), from which we get the term principate for his style of government, and allowing the Senate to confer on him the title of Augustus ("the exalted"), for which reason he is remembered as Caesar Augustus. Still, his constitutional authority over the army was more materially bolstered by his investment of the title of *Imperator* (originally reserved for commanders of victorious Roman armies) with the consular powers of commander in chief, from which evolved the title "emperor." Thus, as both head of state and commander in chief of the army, Caesar Augustus had a double hold over the governor of an imperial province, who, as a *legatus Augustus* (a senior-ranking deputy of the emperor) was his chief provincial magistrate and his provincial military commander in chief.

Caesar Augustus took further precautions by transferring legates at least once every four years, reserving the more sensitive commands to his relatives, and personally controlling all important promotion, rewards, and pay raises in the army. During his reign, the Roman army consisted of 150,000 Roman citizens in twenty-five legions and 150,000 non-citizens in auxiliary infantry cohorts and cavalry regiments, not a large army for an empire that contained, perhaps, sixty million people. But in the east Caesar Augustus relied heavily on client kings and local forces as well as the legions, and, except for four cohorts of the army and the Praetorian Guard (which Caesar Augustus founded), normally no Roman troops were stationed in Italy. Unless the emperor himself was in the field, most of the Praetorian Guard, a force of 9,000 troops, garrisoned Rome in order to safeguard his person.

In the reign of Caesar Augustus, further Roman expansion in the Near East was blocked by Parthia, with its seat of power in Persia (Iran) and its control extending to parts of Mesopotamia and Armenia. The Parthian forces were famous for their mounted bowmen who struck suddenly and then retired before the enemy could counterattack (hence the origin of the expression "a Parthian shot"). The Parthians were the most formidable enemies encountered by the Romans in the first centuries of the Christian era, but other enemies included the Iberian tribes, which periodically kept Spain in turmoil during the two hundred years following the Roman conquest; the Illyrians at the head of the Adriatic who carried out a particularly bloody revolt in the reign of Caesar Augustus; the Dacians located north of the eastern Danube; and the German tribes living east of the Rhine. Regarding the last, when a Roman army of three legions commanded by Publius Quintilius Varus ventured into northern Germany in A.D. 9, German tribesmen led by Hermann (called Armenius by the Romans) ambushed the Roman column while it was marching through the Teutoburger Wald (Teutoburg forest) near modern Detmold. Nearly all of Varus's 20,000 men were killed during two days of fighting. The Romans never occupied more than the fringe areas of Germany.

On the death of Caesar Augustus in A.D. 14, Tiberius, his stepson and an experienced soldier, succeeded him as emperor with the consent of the Senate. A morose and suspicious personality, Tiberius at one point in his reign put down an alleged plot by a prefect of the Praetorian Guard. Perhaps his suspicions were unfounded, but the problem posed by the guard ("who shall guard against the guardians?") was dramatized in the reign of Gaius Caesar, Tiberius's successor and grandson, better known by his nickname Caligula ("Little Boots"). He ascended the throne in 37 only to be stabbed to death in 41 by a tribune of the Praetorian Guard whom he had grossly insulted. The Praetorian Guard then intimidated the Senate into recognizing Tiberius Claudius Caesar (Claudius), Caligula's uncle, as the slain emperor's lawful successor.

In the reign of Claudius (41–54), the Romans invaded Britain, perhaps because of its metals and potential trade, or perhaps because Claudius wanted to be remembered for a conquest. An army under Aulus Plautius overran the southeastern part of the island in 43 and established a Roman capital at Camulodunum (Colchester). But the precarious nature of the Roman foothold in Britain was demonstrated during the reign of Nero (54–68), Claudius's stepson and successor, when in 60 some of the British tribes led by the warrior-queen Boadicea (or Boudica) fell on Camulodunum and the Roman trading center at Londinium (London) and massacred their populations. Only by hard fighting were three Roman legions and their auxiliaries able to put down the revolt. Though the Romans were later able to expand the area of Britain under their control, they never conquered the whole island.

The crisis in Britain had hardly subsided when the Judean Jews rose in revolt in 66, drove the Roman garrison from Jerusalem, and defeated a small Roman army sent from Syria to restore order. Late in 67 Titus Flavianus Vespasianus (Vespasian) was appointed to the command of an army of 50,000 troops for the reconquest of Judea, and during A.D. 68 he recovered most of the country except for Jerusalem and a few fortified places elsewhere. In the same year the bizarre reign of Nero ended with his forced suicide, and there followed civil war among four Roman generals, Vespasian among them, for control of the throne at Rome. After an army under a legate loyal to Vespasian captured Rome and removed his last rival in 69, Vespasian turned over command in Judea to his son Titus and took up his duties as emperor.

The Roman army under Titus in Judea commenced the siege of Jerusalem in 70 in the systematic Roman manner, and, after the defending population had been nearly starved to death, the Romans successfully stormed the city. In the wake of the Roman conquest, many of the Jews were sold into slavery and the Jewish political community was dissolved. (The Diaspora or "pouring out," the dispersal of the Jews over the empire, followed another Jewish revolt in A.D. 115.) Titus turned over the further pacification of Judea to an imperial legate and then variously served his father as perfect of the Praetorian Guard, his father's deputy, and as his co-regent.

Meanwhile, the most dramatic event of the Jewish rebellion took place at Masada, a rocky fortress on a plateau near the Dead Sea. There the last of the Zealots vowed to resist the Roman attacks to the death. A Roman army under Flavius Silva, the new Roman governor of Judea, besieged the fortress and found it necessary to build an earthen rampart thirty stories high in order to approach the walls. On this foundation the Romans built a pier out of boulders and placed on it a siege tower sheathed in iron. From this base they mounted a final attack that breached the Jewish defenses in the spring of A.D. 74. But when the Romans entered Masada, they found not a living soul; rather than surrender, all of the inhabitants had taken each other's lives or committed suicide.

Vespasian was the first emperor "elected" neither by the Senate nor by the Praetorian Guard but by the strongest army in the provinces. He was also the first of the Roman emperors not in some way related to Julius Caesar, a disadvantage he offset by adopting "Caesar" as a title, a practice favored by his successors. He also refilled the nearly empty coffers of the imperial treasury, restored discipline in the army, and established order throughout the empire. By the time of his death in A.D. 79, he well merited his reputation as the "second founder of the principate." Titus, the first natural son to succeed a father to the throne at Rome, continued his father's competent rule but died of fever in 81.

The last of the Flavians was Domitian, Titus's brother, who claimed the title of *dominus* and *deus* ("lord and god"). His lavish spending soon ran the treasury into debt. Still, Domitian can be credited with founding the *castra peregrinorum*, a central army administration that originally dealt with matters of grain supply but eventually widened its duties to include the keeping of officer records and the collection of foreign and domestic intelligence. Domitian was very much a soldier, serving more time in the field with his troops than any previous emperor, but for that reason he was not spared plots in the army. The prefects of the Praetorian Guard were involved in his assassination in 96.

### B. Under the Five Good Emperors

For about eighty years after the death of Domitian, the Roman empire was blessed with the rule in succession of Nerva, Trajan, Hadrian, Antoninus Pius, and Marcus Aurelius—sometimes called the Five Good Emperors. During the reign of Trajan (98–117), Rome launched its last great age of expansion, conquering Dacia beyond the Danube and making it into a bulwark against the restless tribes of the area and, in North Africa, extending its southern frontier of Numidia to the Sahara desert. In Asia, Rome converted the Arabian Nabataea (the area south and east of Jordan and Palestine) into the Roman province of "Arabia." While invading Armenia and Mesopotamia in 114–115, Trajan defeated the Parthians and drove them inside Persia (Iran). When he stood at the head of the Persian Gulf in 116, he had come further east than any Roman general or emperor before or after him. He was about to invade Persia when he fell ill and died in August 117.

During his reign, Trajan had expanded the number of legions to thirty, the number of legionnaires to about 180,000, and the number of auxiliaries to about 200,000. He standardized the arms, armor, and equipment of his army to the point where there was very little difference between the infantry of the legion and those of the auxiliaries. He further diluted the difference with generous grants of citizenship to the auxiliaries so that they could transfer to the legions, and, in consequence, the percentage of Italian soldiers in some of his legions dropped to as low as one percent.

The emperor Hadrian (r. 117–138), a general and Trajan's cousin, abandoned Trajan's policy of expansion in favor of consolidation, centralization, and fortification. Hadrian's Wall, a line of permanent fortifications thrown up in Britain from the mouth of the river Tyne to Solway Firth and delimiting the limits of Roman territory, was perhaps Hadrian's most fitting monument. Permanent fortified camps were also constructed along the Rhine and the Danube, each connected to the next camp and to the interior by excellent paved roads. The imperial armies were permitted to recruit increased numbers of native soldiers from the border provinces, and this policy intensified the trend toward permanent garrisons at the frontiers composed of native troops. Antoninus Pius (r. 138–161) continued his predecessor's policies of conservation with the exception that he authorized a further Roman advance into Britain and the building of a new fortified line between the Firth of Clyde and the Firth of Forth.

While Marcus Aurelius was on the throne (161–180), the Roman empire began to experience serious difficulties. Early in his reign, Parthian forces invaded Armenia, defeated a Roman army, and threatened the whole Ro-

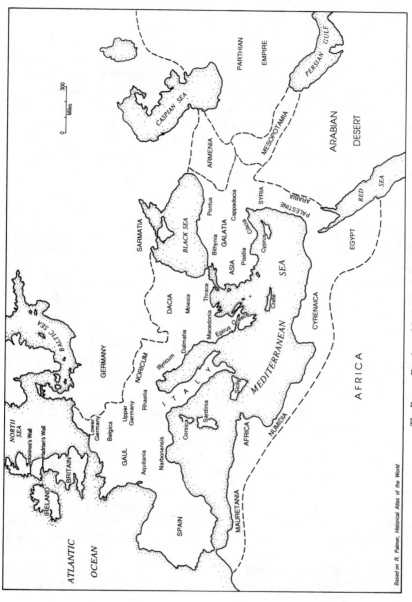

The Roman Empire at Maximum Expansion c. 120 A.D.

man position in Mesopotamia. By the end of 166 upper Mesopotamia had been recovered from the Parthians, but by 169 the empire was dealing with an invasion of the barbarian Quadi and the Marcomanni across Dacia and the Danube. These barbarians penetrated the empire as far as the head of the Adriatic Sea, and, in this crisis, Marcus Aurelius cast aside custom and law in order to fill his legions with any men he could get, including conscripts, foreign mercenaries, and even freed slaves and gladiators. His measures enabled the Romans to drive the barbarians back to the Danube and to defeat them north of the river in 172–173, but the episode was an indication that pressures from without the empire were growing. Moreover, the death of Marcus Aurelius in March 180 marked the passing of the last of the "Five Good Emperors" from the scene.

## C. Militarism and Anarchy

Commodus, Marcus Aurelius's son and heir, proved to be the "ignoble son of a noble father," and, after his assassination in 192, the empire was plunged into internecine strife until the legate Publius Septimius Severus made himself emperor by force of arms. By 197 Severus had restored order to the empire and fended off still another Parthian invasion of Mesopotamia, but, and more clearly than any emperor preceding him, he viewed the army as his ultimate source of authority. He abolished most of the remaining class distinctions in the army, raised its pay by a third, and broke with tradition by stationing a legion in Italy in order to have a central reserve. When he was dying in 211, he advised his son and heir Marcus Aurelius Antoninus (better known as "Caracalla" for the long cloak he affected) to "reward the soldiers and scorn the rest."

Caracalla fairly emptied the Roman treasury following his father's advice, and, in addition, he made all his free male subjects Roman citizens in order to exploit an income tax. The economy of the empire began to bog down from the tax drain on its revenues and the fixation of the emperors on the loyalty of the army. Yet Caracalla was assassinated in 217, and the same fate met the two emperors who followed him. The assassination of Severus Alexander in 235 was followed by a fifty-year struggle to control the throne in Rome, a period far longer than the periods of disorder in 68–69 and 193–197.

Adding to the effects of the growing chaos within the Roman government was the increasing tide of invasion of Roman territory by new waves of barbarians, especially the Goths from eastern Europe. Their threat was first recognized in 250 when, in a raid as far south as Greece, they annihilated a Roman army in Thrace led by the emperor Decius. The empire was also threatened with internal defection, including movements of secession in Gaul, Syria, Egypt, and part of Asia Minor. Though in his short reign (270–275) the emperor Aurelian managed to meet all these crises and thereby earn his boast on his coins that he was "restorer of the world,"

Dacia, north of the Danube, was permanently abandoned, Rome was fortified for the first time since the Punic Wars, and the Imperial Army was so transformed that it hardly resembled the organization founded by Caesar Augustus.

## D. The Final Resurgence

By Aurelian's time, Roman units at the frontiers had taken on the appearance of militia, mobile elements of the army were increasingly mounted in order to move more rapidly from one threatened place to another, and the infantry's javelin and short sword had been replaced by the lance of the mounted soldier and a long sword originally favored by the auxiliaries. The long, oblong shield had been replaced by the handier, round buckler. The new shock cavalry were modeled after the Persian *cataphractarii* (armored, mounted lancers), and a species of mounted archers had been equipped with an Asian compound bow. Aurelian hastened the process of transfer of emphasis to the cavalry during his reign, the cavalry corps being placed on a par with the Praetorian Guard as a *corps d'élite*. Also, the new military title of *dux* (duke) was invented for the commander of specialized field armies, cavalry, or forces grouped in particular areas not corresponding to the old provincial commands.

In Diocletian's reign (285–305), the momentous step was taken of abandoning Rome as the capital and center of the empire. The emperor appointed a fellow augustus (co-emperor) and two caesars (deputy emperors), gave each member of this tetrarchy (rule by four) a part of the empire to defend, and allowed each to set up his headquarters in the city of his choosing. Under this system, and despite the empire's decline in population and wealth, Diocletian managed to support 390,000 troops and a navy manned by 40,000 sailors. But when in 305 Diocletian abdicated and went into retirement—the only Roman emperor ever to do so—civil war broke out, and complete order was not restored until Constantine was victorious over his rivals.

During his reign (305–337), Constantine ordered the building of a new capital on the site of ancient Byzantium at a point where the Bosphorous joins the Sea of Marmara. The location of Constantinople (the "city of Constantine," now Istanbul) at a principal crossing between Europe and Asia and on the strategic trading lanes between the Black Sea and the Mediterranean suggested the increasing dependence of the empire on its sources of food and trade in the east and a relative falling off of importance of the western empire. Constantinople became the official imperial residence in 330.

Constantine also allowed German tribes to settle peacefully within the borders of the empire in return for their supply of soldiers to his army, and in this manner he tried to offset the declining population of the empire. This practice, however, further "barbarized" the army and made the empire more dependent on outside support. He also abolished the Praetorian Guard, ending forever its stormy career of three and a half centuries, and replaced it with a German mounted guard known as the *scholae*, a body of troops originally founded by Diocletian. The old form of the legion entirely disappeared when Constantine applied the term to a mixed unit of 1,500 infantry and cavalry. He also redisignated the leading generals of the army as "master of horse" and "master of foot" respectively. Eventually, the two masters were combined in a "master of soldiers," effectively the commander in chief of the army under the emperor.

### E. The Decline and Fall

A succession of emperors after Constantine failed to bring peace to the empire, and, in 378, while attempting to stop an invasion of Visigoths (West Goths) south of the Danube, the Emperor Valens lost his life when his army was defeated at the battle of Adrianople. In this battle, in which 20,000 out of 30,000 Romans on the field were killed, the mounted Goths first defeated the Roman cavalry, then surrounded the Roman infantry. Some historians have made of this event the beginning of the domination of mounted soldiers over infantry, supposedly characteristic of much of the Middle Ages, but a better case could be made that Adrianople was another example of the mutual dependence between mounted soldiers and soldiers on foot. Actually, most of the barbarians who overwhelmed the late Roman empire in the West fought on foot.

Theodosius I, Valens's successor, made peace with the Visigoths by allowing them to settle in the largely depopulated provinces south of the Danube, though at the cost of further diluting their Roman character. Upon Theodosius's death in 395, the Roman empire was divided between his sons Arcadius and Honorius. As emperor in the West and with a capital at Ravenna in northern Italy, Honorius was forced to withdraw his troops from Britain and the Rhine frontier under the pressure of new Germanic invasions of the western empire in the early 400s. He even proved unable to prevent the Visigoths under Alaric from raiding the Italian peninsula and sacking Rome in 410. Honorius died in 423, and his successor, Valentinian III, was little more than a figurehead. Roman authority, such as it remained in the West, was wielded by Aetius, "master of the soldiers."

With assistance from the Visigoths, Aetius and his army beat back the invasion of Gaul by the Huns under Attila in 451, and the next year confined the Hun's invasion of Italy to the area north of Rome. Attila withdrew his forces beyond the Danube, and, upon his death in 453, the Hunnish empire collapsed. But the Roman West had little time left to it. Aetius was assassinated in 454 and Valentinian III shared this fate in 455. For the next twenty years struggles among the numerous claimants to the throne of the western empire prevented its cohesive defense as Germanic peoples continued to hammer at its fragments. Finally, in the year 476, the German barbarian Odovacar, by then "Master of the Soldiers," deposed the young Emperor Romulus Augustulus and made himself king in Italy. This was the event that the eighteenth-century British historian Edward Gibbon called the "fall" of the Roman empire in the West; actually it was the point where the "Germanization" of the Western empire was completed.

In 493, with the approval of the Eastern emperor Zeno, Theodoric, King of the Ostrogoths, overthrew and killed Odovacar and was rewarded by Zeno with the title of "Governor of Romans and Goths" in the West. But Theodoric's empire would not last, and its ties to the Eastern empire were largely severed by his death in 526. Though the Eastern or Byzantine emperor Justinian made repeated efforts to recover the western territories in Italy and North Africa, after his death in 565 his successors were content to hold onto a few outposts in the western Mediterranean. The West as a whole embarked on a largely separate voyage through the Middle Ages, and in both East and West new patterns of war began to emerge.

## IV. War in India, China, and Japan

One of the stranger technological aspects of history is why it took so long for the stirrup to be developed. The Romans brought the traditional weapons of antiquity to their peak, but their horsemen sat on little more than padded seats and never possessed the stirrup which insures the horseman's stability. Likewise, no previous Mediterranean or Near Eastern culture produced the stirrup. Although authorities differ (some claim that representations of the stirrup, or what appears to be a stirrup, appears in some Buddhist carvings in India as early as 200 B.C.), it is probable that the toe loop, the forerunner of the stirrup, was invented in India sometime in the first century A.D. From India its use spread slowly east and west, gradually evolving into the stirrup as we know it today. The Celts probably invented the horseshoe in the fourth century, and the Byzantines had adopted both the stirrup and horseshoe at least by the late sixth century. Stirrups and horseshoes may not have been in general use in medieval western Europe until a couple of centuries later. The stirrup was especially important to the effectiveness of the Byzantine cataphract in the Eastern Roman empire and the medieval knight in the West.

China disintegrated into a condition of feudal warfare between 403 and 221 B.C., and that time is referred to as one of "warring states." Though chariots remained a powerful striking force in this period, a tough peasant infantry in large numbers also participated, fighting with javelins, short swords, and bows, and the general introduction of iron made Chinese weapons and armor more effective. In 249 B.C. the Chou dynasty was replaced by the Chin, and thereafter the chariot faded from use in favor of cavalry, though it was probably the fifth century A.D. before Chinese cavalry benefited from the stirrup. The Chinese also caught up with the Near

Eastern and Western worlds in the art of siegecraft, their armies including catapults, scaling ladders, and techniques and equipment for tunneling and the building of siege towers.

The Chin dynasty eventually restored order and union to China, and its most remarkable military achievement, beginning with the Chin emperor Shi Huang Ti (r. 246–210 B.C.), was the construction of a line of fortifications across northern China to keep out invasions of nomadic raiders. Subsequent emperors over many centuries used forced labor to expand the line until it finally became the celebrated Great Wall of China. When completed in the seventeenth century A.D., the Great Wall was the longest continuous fortification ever erected. Even today it zig-zags across northern China for 2,500 miles, covering a frontier that measures on a straight line 1,600 miles. Made principally of brick, it is generally twenty-five feet at the base, seventeen feet wide at the crest, and has an average height of three stories (thirty feet). A continuous road, protected on both sides by parapets, runs across the top, punctuated at intervals by guard towers. When properly manned, the Great Wall was a major barrier to nomadic raiders.

Japan's ancient history is almost totally cloaked in legend and tradition, but long before Christ the ancestors of the Japanese are believed to have migrated from the high plateau of Asia across the sea to the islands then occupied by a primitive people known as the Ainu. The Japanese gradually extended their control over the whole island chain, stretching for a thousand miles from north to south, but remained for a long time on a tribal level. They imported Chinese Bronze Age culture by way of Korea, though they retained a distinctive language. In A.D. 100 the Chinese reported that Japanese chieftains were importing iron weapons and armor from China.

Not until the fourth century A.D. were the Japanese on the island of Kyushu able to impose their will on the other Japanese populations and to set up a centralized government at Yamato. Even then there were rebellions and disorders. Still, a distinctive Japanese pattern of war had begun to emerge, centered on the aristocratic knight, elaborately armored and mounted on horseback. His chief weapon was the bow, but he also was armed with the sword. The tradition that warriors were drawn from the upper classes was probably established at this time.

# THREE
■ ■ ■

# War in the Middle Ages

## I. The Byzantine Struggle to Survive

Though the Western Roman empire declined into a condition of semi-barbarism in the sixth century—the onset of the so-called Dark Ages in the Western world—the Eastern Roman or Byzantine empire, or at least a portion of it, managed to survive for nearly a millennium longer. The long Byzantine survival was due in part to the remarkable performance of its army, the basic administrative and tactical unit of which was the *numerus*, about four hundred soldiers commanded by a tribune. The *numeri* were about equally divided by type between infantry and cavalry, but the cavalry were more important.

The heart of the Byzantine army was the cataphract, a missile-shock soldier who functioned from horseback as an armored, mounted lancer or, with his bow, as a mounted archer. His effectiveness was increased by adoption, probably in the late sixth century, of the stirrup, which enabled the cataphract to impart a greater force with his lance in the charge and to achieve a greater accuracy with his bow from the saddle than previous cavalry serving the Roman empire. The cataphract was also well protected by a casque or conical metal helmet, chain-mail armor from his neck to his thighs, and a small shield strapped to his left arm.

The Byzantine cavalry were supported by heavy infantry, each infantryman equipped with a long spear and sword, and the heavy infantry normally massed in phalanxes sixteen ranks deep on the battlefield. Light infantry, armed with bows and javelins, usually accompanied the cavalry and heavy infantry. Five to eight numeri (2,000–3,200 cavalry and infantry) formed a *turma*, two or three turmae (4,000 to 9,600 soldiers) constituted a *thema*, and three or four themae grouped together constituted a Byzantine field army, usually numbering 25,000–30,000 men. Exclusive of local militia, the Byzantine empire probably never had more than 100,000 men under arms at one time, but the mobility and discipline of its troops and the cleverness of its commanders often more than offset its inferior numbers.

In the sixth century, during the reign of Justinian, Byzantine armies under generals such as Belisarius and Narses not only beat off Persian attacks on the eastern frontiers of the empire but they regained parts of Italy and North Africa from the Western barbarian peoples. In the seventh century the greatest threat to Byzantium was posed by the militant advocates of Islam, a religious faith proclaimed by the prophet Mohammed and first adopted by the tribes of Arabia. By the time of the Prophet's death in 632, the Arabs were on the point of unleashing a holy war. Their armies overran Palestine in 634, Syria in 635, and subsequently Mesopotamia, Persia, and Egypt. The Arab advance reached Libya in 650 and Morocco in 700. Muslims known as Moors swept across Spain early in the eighth century and raided far into France until the Franks turned them back at the Battle of Tours in 732 (see below). The chief Arab advantages were their religious fanaticism, numbers, and a splendid light cavalry armed with scimitar and bow.

The Byzantine empire warded off repeated Muslim attacks on its eastern frontiers in the seventh century, but in the next century it nearly succumbed to a Muslim invasion that by August 717 had brought the enemy before the walls of Constantinople. Perhaps 200,000 strong, the Muslim army besieged the city for a year, but the Byzantine troops threw back all the Muslim assaults and vigorously defended their capital with the help of catapults and "Greek fire," a Byzantine secret weapon. Greek fire was apparently produced by some mixture of sulphur, naphtha, and quicklime, and, when ignited and poured down from the walls on assaulting troops, or projected by flamethrowers in some way utilizing water pressure, it could be as searing as today's napalm. Even some of the Byzantine ships were equipped with the flamethrowing device. The battered and singed Muslims finally abandoned their effort against Constantinople, and only 30,000 of them survived the retreat to their own territory. The Byzantine victory at Constantinople was followed by Byzantine reoccupation of Anatolia and the establishment of a more secure frontier in the east against future attacks.

Over the next two centuries the Byzantine empire actually expanded as its armies seized territories in the Balkans, Asia Minor, Syria, and Armenia. Then, in 1071, it experienced a defeat that marked the beginning of an irreversible decline in its fortunes. In that year Seljuk Turks under Alp Arslan seized the town of Manzikert (located to the northeast of Lake Van and near the present-day border of Turkey and Iran), and Emperor Romanus IV Diogenes led an army of 40,000 Byzantine troops to its relief. On the day of battle, the Turkish army prudently withdrew before it could be decisively engaged, but the cataphracts, in their pursuit of the retiring Turks, became separated from their supporting infantry. At dusk Romanus IV Diogenes ordered his cavalry and infantry to rejoin forces, but some of his infantry disobeyed his orders to advance and the movement of other units became confused by darkness. The Turks, who had followed the retreating cataphracts, seized the opportunity to launch a fierce attack, and the army of Romanus IV Diogenes, caught divided, was nearly annihilated.

In the wake of the loss of nearly half of the Byzantine army at Manzikert, the Seljuk Turks seized much of Anatolia and the Levant, including the cities of Antioch, Damascus, and Jerusalem. Deprived of territory from which it drew much of its manpower and the horses for its cavalry, the Byzantine army declined in effectiveness. Though Byzantine appeals in the late eleventh century to the West for military assistance helped to spark the Crusades, even these rebounded against its long-term interests. In 1204, during the Fourth Crusade, the Venetians conquered Constantinople, installed their own candidate on the throne, and, until 1261, ruled a Latin kingdom that stretched from Greece to Asia Minor. Even after Byzantine autonomy was reestablished, the empire remained weak, and the last remnant was extinguished when the Ottoman Turks captured Constantinople in 1453.

## II. Frankish Dominance and Charlemagne

The warriors who brought down the Western Roman empire in the fifth and sixth centuries were never very numerous. Studies have shown that the principal barbarian peoples could not have fielded more than 30,000 warriors apiece, some of them no more than 10,000. Moreover, excepting the Ostrogoths, they used very rudimentary tactics. The favorite tactic of the Germanic warriors on foot was to form a massive wedge in order to break through opposing lines by sheer impetus and concentration. Armed with battle axes, long swords, and spears, and protected by a modicum of body armor and helmets, their strength lay not in clever tactics but in their reckless courage and warrior spirit. As for overcoming fortified places, most of the time they were unable to build, let alone use, the siege weapons of

The Norman Conquest of England, 1066

the day. However, the old fortifications in the West had declined through neglect, and many towns and cities were too depopulated to offer much resistance.

Though the barbarian peoples within the former empire gradually ceased their migratory behavior, they remained organized for war, and every able-bodied freeman was obligated to serve in the warrior host. In their highly decentralized kingdoms, the function of the king was primarily that of war lord. These barbarian kingdoms often adopted Roman terminology to designate positions of political and military leadership: the king's principal military chiefs were designated as dukes, and, in turn, their chief military subordinates were called counts, both ranks being directly drawn from the armies of the late Roman empire, though reversed in importance. Chosen by the king from the wealthier and more prominent men of the kingdom, dukes and counts presided over duchies and counties into which the kingdom was divided for administrative and military purposes.

The most powerful of the western kingdoms in the Dark Ages was that of the Franks, a Germanic people, who by 481 occupied the territory that is today the Netherlands, Belgium, and northern France, and whose name is the origin of the word France. In 496 the Frankish king Clovis and his subjects were converted to the form of Christianity championed by the Bishop of Rome (later the Pope or "father" of the Western church), and the Roman church's influence was further spread when Clovis crushed the independence of the Visigoth kingdom in southwestern France in 507. Four years later Clovis created a national kingdom that stretched across France to the Pyrenees. Eventually, a succession of weak Frankish kings of the Merovingian dynasty led to the practice of real power being wielded by a royal official known as the mayor of the palace. By the middle of the seventh century, Frankish government was so decentralized that dukes and counts viewed their positions as no longer appointive but hereditary, and, accordingly, a self-perpetuating noble class began to emerge. Most peasant farmers lost their lands to the nobility and became serfs, and, by the end of the seventh century, only about ten per cent of the Frankish farmers were still free-holders.

Still, the tradition of the warrior host was alive enough in the early eighth century that when 20,000 Moorish cavalry from Spain raided France in 732, Charles Martel, mayor of the palace, was able to form an infantry host capable of defeating the Moors at the battle of Tours. The Franks fought in a massive square, repeatedly fending off the Moorish mounted attacks in what turned out to be the last victory of the old Frankish host. In the wake of their defeat at Tours, the Moors withdrew to southern France and, in 759, finally withdrew across the Pyrenees into Spain.

After the battle of Tours, the effectiveness of mounted soldiers over infantry began to predominate even among the Franks. This development was not due solely to technical factors such as the stirrup; it was also due to the fact that the nobility could better afford weapons, armor, and time to train the infantry, drawn as they were, from a debased peasant population. Charles Martel himself may have begun the process of creating feudal cavalry in the West when he recruited a body of mounted soldiers whom he rewarded with sufficient land to enable each soldier to maintain himself, his equipment, and a number of horses suitable for war. The exchange of land for pledges of military service (vassalage) began a system of feudalism among the nobility that gradually made the mounted man-at-arms the backbone of medieval armies in the West.

Pepin the Short supplanted the last of the Merovingian kings in 752, and his son Charlemagne ("Charles the Great"), who ruled from 771 to his death in 814, was the greatest of the Carolingian dynasty and the Frankish monarchs. He brought a degree of centralization to the administration and control of the Frankish empire unknown before his time and expanded his empire through war until it encompassed nearly all the West, save most of Spain, North Africa, southern Italy, and Britain. Beginning in 782, Charles established seven frontier provinces (known as marks or marches and ruled by margraves) as buffers between his territories and alien lands. Behind those buffers the empire was divided into more than three hundred counties, grouped in duchies, and from his capital at Aachen (Aix-la-Chapelle), Charlemagne ruled his empire through *missi dominici* (royal envoys) bearing capitularies (royal ordinances) to his subordinates. Five capitularies issued between 803 and 813 set forth the duties of the Carolingian vassals in raising forces, the property basis for military call ups, how units were to be organized, and specifying the number and condition of horses, weapons, armor, and other equipment. Though in practice the Carolingian empire never fielded at one time more that 20,000 horsemen and 30,000 infantry, theoretically it could mobilize up to 35,000 mounted men-at-arms and 100,000 foot soldiers. Charlemagne's dominance in the West became so great that in the year 800 the Pope crowned him "Emperor of the Romans."

### III. From Charlemagne to the Norman Conquest

#### A. The New Barbarian Invasions

Charlemagne died in 814 and with him went the unity of the West. His heirs quarreled and, after 840, his former empire was divided into West Frankland (most of western France), Lotharingia (a kingdom stretching from the Netherlands in the north to central Italy in the south), and East Frankland (an area roughly corresponding to the territory of West Germany today). Lotharingia disintegrated, and its major parts—Lorraine in the north and Burgundy and part of Italy in the south—were causes for wars between German and French monarchs for centuries to come. Though Otto the Great managed to get control of the unruly duchies of East Frankland in the tenth century, and the Pope crowned him Emperor Otto I in 962, his empire consisted of only parts of Germany and Italy. West Frankland, or France, began to emerge as a separate power in 887 when the nobility elected Odo, Count of Paris, as their king. He and succeeding monarchs of France remained independent of the German emperors.

Western Europe was not only plagued with division after Charlemagne's death, it was also threatened by new barbarian threats. The Magyars— swift-riding, Asiatic raiders armed chiefly with the bow—periodically invaded Germany until feudal forces under Otto I defeated them at the Battle of the Lech (Lechfeld) in 955. The Magyars finally settled down to dominate an empire in Hungary and converted to Christanity. A more sustained threat was offered by the Vikings, or Norsemen, terms for a variety of Scandinavian warrior peoples, including the Danes, Norwegians, Swedes, Varangians, Normans, and still others.

The Vikings used their famous "long ships," essentially galley craft, to carry them on vast raiding and colonizing expeditions throughout the Baltic, the North Sea, and as far south as the Mediterranean. Those Vikings called Normans established states in France, Sicily, and southern Italy, and they repeatedly threatened the Byzantine empire from the west. The Varangians penetrated deeply into many parts of eastern Europe by way of the river networks, some of them driving down the Volga river in Russia and conquering Slavic populations as far south as the Caspian Sea.

Much earlier, as the Western Roman empire was collapsing in the late fifth and early sixth centuries, the Germanic Angles and Saxons invaded southern Britain, drove out part of the Celtic population and dominated the rest. (The word "England" is a corruption of "Angleland.") But the Anglo-Saxon kingdoms established in Britain warred among themselves, and they were subject to periodic invasions of Danish and Norwegian Vikings. The Danelaw remained a Viking territory in England until the late ninth century, when Alfred the Great finally brought it under Saxon control. Alfred is also credited with the founding of the first English navy when in 875 he had relatively large, galley-style vessels built in order to intercept future Viking invasions at sea. Athelstan, Alfred's grandson, used Alfred's fleet, as well as his army, to subdue the rest of Britain early in the tenth century, the first time that the whole island was brought under one rule.

Under the impact of internal revolt and more Viking invasions, Saxon dominance in Britain collapsed in the reign of King Ethelred the Unready, and between 1017 and 1035 King Canute ruled England as part of an empire that also included Denmark and Norway. Saxon England regained its independence after the death of Canute, but its military institutions continued to reflect Viking influences; thus, the Housecarls—a royal body guard of a thousand men founded in Canute's reign—continued to serve the Saxon monarchs, and, in time of war, the Saxon king relied on an army composed of Housecarls, earls (feudal nobility), thanes (professional warriors), and the fyrd, a host of commoners mobilized in time of emergency. Like the Vikings, the Saxons used the horse primarily for transportation and usually fought on foot with battle axe, sword, spear, javelin, and the short bow.

In 912 the King of France purchased a measure of relief from Viking ravages by granting a duchy on the western coast to a chieftain called Rolf (or Rollo), the duchy subsequently called Normandy after its Norse occupiers. Normandy retained its independence and eventually became the most centralized duchy in France. Moreover, by the mid-eleventh century and the rule of William, the seventh Duke of Normandy, Norman military institutions had progressed beyond those of the Saxons, Vikings, and rival French. In war, William relied heavily on a combination of mounted knights clad in chain-mail armor and wielding swords and lances, and on experienced mercenary infantry armed with the spear and the short bow. His feudal-mercenary army was a well balanced, shock-missile force, perhaps more advanced for its time that any other in western Europe. Thus, William was able to triumph over French feudal rivals, prevent Normandy's absorption into the Kingdom of France, and ultimately carry out a successful invasion of Saxon England.

### B. The Norman Conquest of England

When the Saxon king Edward the Confessor died in January 1066, both William of Normandy, Edward's distant cousin, and Harold Hardrada ("Harold the Ruthless"), the Viking king of Norway and a descendant of Canute, claimed the right of succession to the English throne. Both were outraged when the Witan, the Anglo-Saxon council, passed over their claims and awarded the English throne to Harold Godwinsson, the powerful Saxon Earl of Wessex. Even the Saxons were divided by Harold Godwinsson's succession, Harold's brother Tostig throwing his support to the Viking Harold. Both Harold Hardrada and William of Normandy began assembling armies and fleets, and the Saxon Harold had little choice but to allow his enemies to make the first move and then concentrate his forces appropriately for the defense of his realm.

Harold Godwinsson's strategy was first tested when Harold Hardrada's army of perhaps 8,000 Viking warriors, accompanied by Tostig, invaded northern England in the late summer of 1066, marched to the vicinity of York, and on September 20 defeated a local force of earls, thanes, and fyrd at the Battle of Gate Fulford. After King Harold learned of the invasion of the north in his capital in London, he put himself at the head of a mounted force of Housecarls, earls, and thanes, and commenced a march that covered two hundred miles in five days. Meanwhile, Harold Hardrada's army camped a few miles from York around Stamford Bridge, over the river Derwent. Members of the local fyrd had joined King Harold's army by the time it approached the Viking camp on September 25, perhaps making its numbers equal to those under Harold Hardrada, but, in any case, the sudden appearance of Godwinsson's army took the Vikings by surprise. In the bitter Battle of Stamford Bridge that followed, the Vikings experienced the worst defeat they ever suffered on English soil, and both Harold Hardrada and Tostig were killed. King Harold allowed the Viking survivors to return to Norway.

Harold Godwinsson's army was still near York and celebrating its victory over Harold Hardrada's army when on October 1 it learned that four days earlier a Norman army under Duke William had landed at Pevensey Bay on the southern coast of England. After dismissing the local fyrd, Harold and his mounted retainers commenced a forced march back to London, and after learning in London that William's army—consisting of perhaps 1,500 knights and 5,000 other soldiers—had built a fortified camp on the coast at Hastings sixty miles away, Harold ordered mobilization of the southern fyrd. It was still assembling, however, when Harold left London on October 11 with a force of undisclosed numbers in a march toward Hastings, and perhaps he planned to assemble his army, including the fyrd, just beyond the forest of the Weald and near Senlac Ridge not far from Hastings and then surprise William by a sudden attack on his camp as he had defeated Harold Hardrada in the previous campaign.

If this was Harold's plan, matters did not work out as he expected. Probably no more than 7,000 men had joined him on Senlac Ridge by the morning of October 14 when, about the ninth hour, the Norman army, having left its camp hours before, appeared before the Saxon position. Thus, at the beginning of the somewhat mislabeled Battle of Hastings, Harold had lost the initiative and may have been outnumbered. Certainly, the quality of William's army was generally better than that of the Saxons'.

Harold's troops proceeded to form a "shield-wall," the Housecarls and thanes surrounding the king at the center of the Saxon line, and the rest of the army, mostly composed of fyrd, massed on the flanks. William wasted no time in ordering an attack on the Saxon position with spearmen and bowmen, following up these infantry attacks with charges by mounted men at arms. As the Saxons had the advantage of occupying the higher ground, they were able to beat back the earlier Norman attacks with their spears, axes, and javelins. The battle raged indecisively until the Saxons finally committed a fatal tactical blunder. After the Normans had recoiled in some disorder following one of their unsuccessful attacks, some of the Saxons rushed after them in order to exploit their advantage. On the flat, the Saxons were vulnerable to William's cavalry, which proceeded to charge them until they were annihilated. The loss of this body of troops weakened the numbers and resolve of the remaining Saxons, and the Norman cavalry managed to get a foothold on the ridge late in the day. From their new position, the Norman cavalry charged the Saxons with ever greater effect, and what hope remained for the Saxon cause vanished when Harold was first struck in the eye by an arrow and then was cut down by a Norman sword. Soon after the rest of the demoralized Saxons fled the

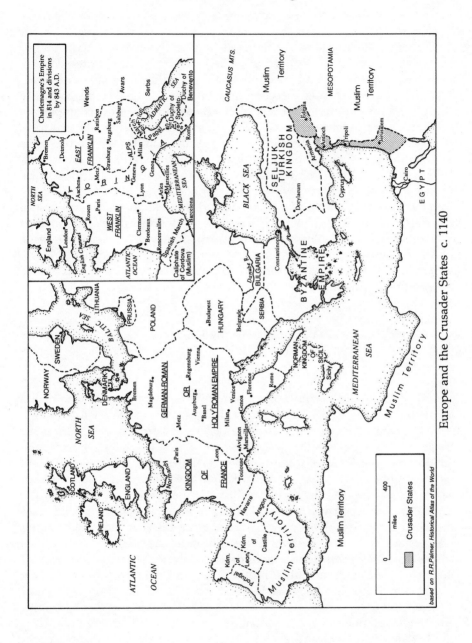

Europe and the Crusader States c. 1140

based on R.R.Palmer, *Historical Atlas of the World*

Crusader States

battlefield. William of Normandy emerged from the fray as William the Conqueror.

The complete conquest of England was not, however, immediately achieved through the victory at Senlac Ridge (Hastings), for scattered Saxon resistance continued until 1069, and by then a third of the country had been devastated. During the conquest, William compelled the Witan to recognize him as king, ordered a Norman castle built in every important borough, and appointed a vassal to serve in each district as his governor. He was careful to take title to the whole of the country and to make his vassals swear an oath of personal loyalty to him in return for their fiefs. William thus insured that the Norman form of centralized feudalism replaced the loose-knit patchwork of earldoms that had dominated the political and military forms of Saxon England. He also extended his control to Scotland in 1072, and later on he returned to Normandy in order to deal with other enemies. William finally died of an injury sustained at the Battle of Mantes, thirty miles from Paris, in 1087. His Anglo-French empire survived, however, and with profound consequences for Britain and France for centuries to come.

## IV. The Age of the Crusades

### A. The First Crusade

In the late eleventh century the Byzantine Emperor Alexius I Comnenus appealed to Pope Urban II to use his influence in the West for the dispatching of military aid in order to assist the emperor in recovering his Asiatic districts. Urban II seized upon this request to justify a much more ambitious project, namely the recovery of Palestine—the so-called Holy Land—from control of the Seljuk Turks and the Saracens (the latter a term loosely applied to the Arab peoples of Syria, Lebanon, Palestine, and the Trans-Jordan). At a church council at Clermont in November 1095, Urban preached a sermon that opened a vein of enthusiasm not only among prelates and nobles, but among the common folk as well.

The forces of the First Crusade were principally led by a half dozen French nobles—Hugh of Vermandois, brother of King Philip I of France, Robert of Normandy (the brother of King William II of England), Bohemond and Tancred, Norman lords from southern Italy, Raymond of Toulouse and Godfrey of Bouillon. Their 4,500 knights and 30,000 infantry, plus thousands of religious pilgrims, swarmed into Constantinople in 1096, and in the spring of 1097 set off on a march across Anatolia. In June they successfully besieged Nicea (now Iznik in Turkey), the Seljuk capital, and were not seriously challenged in the field until they had pushed deeper into Anatolia at the beginning of July.

As the Crusaders were advancing through Anatolia in two forces about equal in size and a day's march apart, an army of 40,000 Seljuk Turks commanded by Kilij Arslan I fell on the force commanded by Bohemond near Dorylaeum. Bohemond sent for help, but for six hours his troops had to endure repeated Turkish attacks and a rain of arrows from the powerful Turkish bows. Christian counter attacks with heavy cavalry proved fruitless against the agile Turkish light cavalry, which faded away before the charges and then returned to the attack after the Christian knights had retired to Bohemond's position. Just when the strength of Bohemond's men was almost at an end, knights from the second column rode up to strike the Turks in the rear and to drive them from the battlefield. About 3,000 Turks and 4,000 Crusaders fell in the fighting, but Dorylaeum was the first battlefield victory claimed by the Crusaders.

After completing their march across Asia Minor, the forces of the First Crusade split into two groups, the one under Baldwin of Boulogne and Tancred going on to establish Christian rule over Edessa in Armenia in March 1098, the other to commence a march down the eastern coast of the Mediterranean toward Jerusalem. The army marching on Jerusalem nearly starved before capturing Antioch in June 1098, and by the time it stood before Jerusalem in mid-June 1099, its fighting strength consisted of only 1,200 knights and 11,000 infantry.

Nevertheless, under the direction of Godfrey of Bouillon, the Crusaders commenced a siege, built three siege towers, and launched assaults on Jerusalem's defenses. After hard fighting, the Crusaders finally penetrated the walls on the night of July 13, and then spent the next two days putting an estimated 70,000 Muslims and Jews to the sword. The Crusaders confirmed their grip on Jerusalem in August when they defeated a relieving army from Egypt at the battle of Ascalon (Ashkelon).

### B. The Muslim Counter-Crusade

Godfrey of Bouillon ruled Jerusalem with the title of Advocate of the Holy Sepulchre until his death in 1100, then was succeeded by his brother who assumed the title of Baldwin I, King of Jerusalem. The Crusader States eventually consisted of the Kingdom of Jerusalem, the Principality of Antioch, the County of Edessa in Armenia, and the County of Tripoli in Lebanon. Though by the death of Baldwin I in 1118 most of Palestine and part of Syria were under Christian control, as early as 1101 the Seljuk Turks had severed the land-bridge to Constantinople by way of Anatolia, and thereafter most supplies and reinforcements from the West had to come to the Crusader States by sea. The Crusader States tried to offset their lack of manpower and light cavalry by hiring Turcopoles, renegade Muslims, who served them as mounted archers and other types of light cavalry.

The first effective Muslim counter-crusade was led by the Seljuk Turk Zengi, whose army overran Edessa in 1144. His victory provoked Pope Eugenius III to preach the Second Crusade, an effort organized by Bernard of Clairvaux and joined by King Louis VII of France and the German emperor Conrad. Zengi was dead by the time Christian armies assembled at Nicea in Anatolia, but, under Zengi's son Nur ed-Din, the Turkish grip on Armenia proved unshakable, and the Second Crusade was a failure. By 1169 Nur ed-Din's forces were threatening the remaining Crusader States from the north and east, while those of Saladin, his nephew and deputy, threatened them from the direction of Egypt. After Nur ed-Din died in 1174, Saladin became the greatest of the Muslim generals, and was the author of a major disaster that befell the Crusaders.

In 1187 Saladin's army besieged Tiberias on the Sea of Galilee, and Guy of Lusignan, then King of Jerusalem, stripped the defenses of Jerusalem and other cities held by the Crusaders in order to assemble 1,200 knights, 2,000 light cavalry, and 10,000 infantry at Acre for a relief expedition to Tiberias. The Crusader army suffered terribly from heat and thirst on the march through desert country, and, before it could reach its objective, Saladin surrounded it with 20,000 Saracens on high ground known as the Horns of Hattin, about three miles from the Sea of Galilee. Guy's infantry made a desperate effort to reach the Sea of Galilee only to be separated from the cavalry and slaughtered by Turkish arrows. Guy's cavalry was also surrounded and, though some of the Christian knights managed to break through the encirclement and escape to Acre, most, like Guy, were either killed or taken prisoner. Guy, who survived the battle, was later released, but his military reputation was shattered by the disaster at Hattin.

In the wake of their victory at Hattin, Saladin's Saracens captured Tiberias, Acre, and Jerusalem, and by 1188 only Tyre and Antioch remained in the hands of the Crusaders. The news of the fall of Jerusalem, however, gave new force to Pope Gregory VIII's pleas to the Western world for another crusade, the Third. The German emperor Frederick I Barbarossa (Redbeard)—the first to style his domains the "Holy Roman Empire" and himself as "Holy Roman Emperor"—led an army into Anatolia in 1190 in an attempt to open the land route to the Holy Land, but he died in a drowning accident in Cilicia and his army subsequently disintegrated. Only a thousand of his men lived to reach Acre.

### C. Richard vs. Saladin

In the wake of Frederick I's failure, Richard I of England—the "Lionhearted"—made an alliance with Philip II of France for a joint expedition by sea to restore crusader fortunes in the Holy Land. The Anglo-French force of perhaps 30,000 men recovered Acre in July 1191, but quarrels between Richard and Philip caused the latter to return to France, and Richard assumed responsibility for leading the army to recover Jerusalem. As Richard and Saladin were possibly the best generals of the Crusades, their campaigns against each other in 1191–1192 demonstrated the considerable skill of both commanders.

Richard sought to counter the Saracen tactics of provoking fruitless charges and using bowmen to wear down Christian resistance by effective counter measures. Richard's tactics were demonstrated at the Battle of Arsouf (1191) when he placed his archers in the first line, backed them with pike-armed infantry and some dismounted knights, and kept the remainder of his men-at-arms in reserve for commitment at a favorable moment. He also used his Turcopole light cavalry to protect his army's flanks. Richard's deployment at Arsouf suggests that he understood the importance of mutually supporting arms. Unfortunately, in the case of the Battle of Arsouf, he had difficulty with the independent spirit of his knights, some of whom charged the enemy prematurely, and the battle ended in a standoff.

But if Saladin was able to rebuff Richard's drive on Jerusalem, his forces could not prevent the Crusaders from capturing nearly the whole of the Palestinian coastline, including the port of Joppa. By September 1192 both leaders recognized that they had reached a deadlock. Accordingly, they agreed to a truce of five years and an arrangement whereby Jerusalem would remain under Saracen control but Christian pilgrims would have free access to its religious shrines. In return, the Crusaders would permit Muslim traders free access to the ports on the Palestinian coastline. After making these arrangements, Richard sailed from Palestine in October and died while waging war in France before the end of the year; Saladin died in 1193.

### D. The Later Crusades

The end of the Third Crusade closed the golden age of crusading. None of the later Crusades were very distinguished, the Fourth, as mentioned earlier, ending up with the Venetians falling on Constantinople in 1204. The Fifth Crusade was led by a papal legate who botched an invasion of Egypt in 1219, and in the Sixth Crusade, Frederick II, the Holy Roman Emperor and grandson of Frederick Barbarossa, made more progress by the marriage bed than the battlefield. He married the heiress to the Kingdom of Jerusalem, and concluded a treaty with the Saracens in 1229 that placed Jerusalem under Christian control but allowed Muslim and Christian alike freedom of access to the religious shrines of the city. As King of Jerusalem, Frederick scandalized European opinion by visiting both Christian and Muslim shrines before returning to Italy, and he was excommunicated twice by the Pope, both before and after his expedition to the Holy Land.

Within fifteen years of Frederick's departure from the Holy Land, the Khwarisimian Turks, successors to the Seljuks, rampaged through Syria and Palestine, capturing Jerusalem in 1244. (Jerusalem would not be ruled again by Christians until the British occupied it in December 1917, during World War I.) At the council of Lyons in 1245, Pope Innocent IV commissioned Louis IX, King of France, to launch the Seventh Crusade and rescue Jerusalem by way of Egypt, but in 1249 Louis's army was defeated near Cairo. Though Louis survived the defeat and lived to lead the Eighth Crusade, he died of disease in 1270 near Tunis in still another unsuccessful expedition. Meanwhile, Baibars, the Mameluke Sultan of Egypt, had launched a new Muslim effort to drive the Crusaders from the Holy Land, and by 1268 his forces had taken Antioch. His greatest military achievement came, however, in 1271 when his troops took the stupendous fortress of Krak des Chevaliers, perhaps the finest and largest castle ever built by the Crusaders. The death of Baibars in 1277 granted the remaining Christian strongholds in the Holy Land a respite, but the new Egyptian sultan conquered Tripoli in 1289, and, in 1291, he delivered the final blow by taking Acre, the last remnant of the Crusader States. The Age of the Crusades had lasted not quite two hundred years.

### E. Patterns of War during the Crusades

The patterns of war in the Age of the Crusades demonstrated again that even in the Middle Ages—the so-called long age of cavalry—balanced forces operating in mutual support were superior to those that excelled in only one arm. At the beginning of the Crusades, the Christian armies were chiefly strong in heavy cavalry for shock action but lacked the missile power that the Turks enjoyed through light cavalry armed with bows. The Turks, on the other hand, at first lacked good heavy cavalry for shock action. Both sides discovered the need for balanced forces, infantry providing a base of maneuver for the mounted arms, missile support, and a haven for men and mounts exhausted from fighting.

In the Third Crusade, the strength of the Christian infantry was increased by the use of crossbowmen, usually deployed before the pole-armed troops, and knights sometimes dismounted to add their lances to the pikes of the infantry. The Turcopoles were also useful to the crusading armies as missile-armed light cavalry. Thus, the best armies of the Crusades, Christian and Muslim alike, were balanced forces, and the best of the generals— such as Saladin and Richard I—used relatively sophisticated tactics requiring coordinated action by all arms. In addition, both sides became expert in siege warfare and the building of fortified places, the Western soldiers learning much about permanent fortifications by studying the more sophisticated works of the Byzantines, Turks, and Saracens.

## V. Medieval Warfare at Zenith

### A. The Feudal Knight

The typical road to knighthood for a noble son began as early as seven years of age when he was sent to the household of a noble relative or his father's suzerain where he became a page. While serving in that capacity, he was also taught the rudiments of religion, reading and writing, hunting, hawking, and manners. At about sixteen years of age, he was made a squire to a knight, and, in return for the faithful performance of his duties— which included taking care of his knight's mounts and armor—he was taught horsemanship and the uses of the lance, sword, and mace.

At age twenty-one the squire was old enough to be knighted, and by the twelfth century the church insisted in playing a role in the ceremony. The candidate for knighthood bathed before the consecration to symbolize purity, then performed an all-night vigil before the church altar with his armor and weapons. During the mass of the following morning, the priest blessed his sword, whereupon the candidate's lord took the sword, touched the candidate lightly on the shoulder (the accolade) and raised him as a knight recognized. The knight swore an oath of vassalage to the lord and pledged to be faithful to God and to his honor.

The uses of various devices to identify the wearer of knightly armor dated back as far as the ninth century, but by the twelfth century a regular system of markings (called heraldry) had been adopted by European noble families. Medieval artists invented no fewer than 285 basic variations. Shields and breastplates were often decorated with representations of real and fictitious animals, and certain of the knightly Crusaders had the privilege of wearing a sleeveless white shirt marked with a large red cross over their armor. A noble's social position was clearly indicated in his coat of arms, and heralds were responsible for insuring that the proper forms of recognition and order of precedence were observed.

The castle was the center of the noble's life, and was at the same time the residence of the lord and his family and the local administrative and military center. The *donjon,* or central structure, was the focal point of the castle, and was surrounded by storerooms, workshops, and the chapel. A common dining area was provided by the great hall, where entertainments as well as eating took place. Though the great hall had a huge fireplace and a giant table for all to gather round, most rooms in a castle were small, dark, unheated and lit only by torches. Bachelors often slept in the great hall. The average noble entertained himself with the hunt, the joust (a mock combat between two knights), and the tournament (groups of knights in mock battle). Not infrequently, knights were killed or injured in this rough play.

### B. Castles, Fortifications, and Siegecraft

The earliest western European medieval forts and castles, dating back to the ninth century, were crude structures, composed mostly of earth and timbers. Most were constructed according to the "motte and bailey" principle. The motte (mound) might be a hill, a mountain crag, or other relatively high ground, around which it was practical to dig a palisaded ditch or moat. Beyond the motte, a larger area known as the bailey was also surrounded by a ditch with a palisade and became the outer defense of the "castle." Causeways connected the motte to the bailey, and the bailey to the countryside. Usually, the residence of the lord was the first structure in the castle to be converted from earth and timbers to stone. As gates and drawbridges were constructed to obstruct the causeways, stone walls replaced the original palisades of wood. Square towers were constructed at intervals along the outer walls and the walls of the donjon, but, as the influence of the Crusades took hold, the Europeans imitated the Turkish preference for circular towers, which were easier to defend. The original motte evolved into the castle's keep or citadel, the innermost and strongest part of the castle's defenses. As most people imagine it today, the medieval castle was a product of the thirteenth and fourteenth centuries, and designed after Byzantine and Muslim influences had taken hold.

The size of medieval castles varied with their purpose, the means of the owner, and the availability of labor and building materials, but even the largest would have been hard-pressed to shelter more than a few hundred people. Accordingly, as the number and size of towns and cities began to grow in the High Middle Ages, town dwellers raised their own walls and defenses. The growing military independence of the town in matters of defense had a direct relationship to the growing political independence of the bourgeoisie (literally the "city dwellers" but implying a middle class of merchants and artisans) and posed a threat to the authority of the landed aristocracy. In contrast, as long as the rural peasant population remained dependent on feudal protection, it had to tolerate a condition of subservience to the local nobility. Thus, as city-states reappeared in Italy during the Italian Renaissance, feudalism declined more rapidly there than in areas of Europe where urban redevelopment was slower to take hold.

As the defenses of feudal castles and medieval towns and cities became more complex and better constructed, the problem of laying siege to them increased. Medieval armies revived the siege weapons of the ancient world but broke new ground with the trebuchet or mangonel. First mentioned in medieval chronicles in 1147, the trebuchet was used to hurl large stones at walls, but whereas the catapult used tension or torsion for kinetic energy, the propelling force of the trebuchet was provided by a counterweight. A trebuchet with a fifty-foot-long arm and a ten-ton counterweight could hurl a three-hundred-pound stone three hundred yards, and smaller stones still further. The importance of overcoming the fixed defenses of castle or town speedily was increased by the rudimentary logistics of the typical medieval array, which normally made it unsuited for very long sieges. With the onset of winter, the besieging army was usually compelled to break up in order to find food and shelter.

### C. Special Military Orders

The various military-religious orders of Christian knights were formed between the beginning of the twelfth century and the early thirteenth, and together they composed a very special form of medieval military force. The Templars *(fratres militae Templi)* appeared in the Holy Land around 1118 and were at first a group of pious and devout knights commanded by Hugh de Payens, a Burgundian, and Geoffroi de Saint-Omer, a Fleming. The original purpose of the order was to insure the safety of religious pilgrims on the highways of the Crusader states. The Templars eventually expanded their duties to include the recitation of canonical offices in the church of the Temple at Jerusalem (hence the title of Templars), and they became aspirants to religious perfection, taking the triple vow of chastity, poverty and obedience. When at war with the Muslims, they were in the forefront of combat, attested by the fact that no fewer than five Masters of the Temple, as well as a majority of the knights Templar, died, sword in hand, in the century after the order was established.

The Order of the Hospitallers of St. John of Jerusalem, founded in 1137, was similar to that of the Templars, though its origins began with a hospice that provided shelter for pilgrims and many of the early Hospitallers were knights from Spain. The Teutonic Order *(Domus hopitalis sanctae Mariae Teutonicorium)*, most of whose members were German, was founded in 1128 at Jerusalem as a hospital confraternity. The confraternity converted itself into a military order late in the twelfth century, and, after Hermann von Salza, the fourth Master of the Order (1210–1239), became convinced that the Holy Land would fall under Muslim control eventually, he secured territory from the Bishop of Prussia in 1230 where the Order might repair. Eventually, the Order added Livonia and Courland on the Baltic Sea, and its frequent war with Poles and Russians helped to reinforce the traditional enmity between Germans and Slavs.

### D. Medieval Warfare at Zenith, 1150–1336

Between 1150 and 1336, medieval warfare reached its zenith, but there was relatively less internal feuding in this period than in the preceding centuries. This was especially true for France, whose royal and princely authorities made some progress in discouraging private warfare among the feudal nobility. Between 1250 and 1300, the Duchy of Brittany experienced only one war of any length, and Brittany's experience was not exceptional. England knew only twenty years of war during the fifty-six years of Henry III's reign (1216–1272), and only six of those years saw war on English soil. On the other hand, international conflicts—aside from those of the Crusades—were sometimes formidable. The army of Philip Augustus (Philip II), King of France, crushed the armies of an alliance between England's King John and the German emperor Otto IV at the Battle of Bouvines (1214), which had great consequences. The French victory not only ended the danger of a strong German emperor and thereby secured the military predominance of France in western Europe, the outcome so weakened the position of John in England that his barons were able to extort the *Magna Carta*—the foundation of modern English liberties—at Runnymede in 1215.

Before and during the Crusades most knights wore chain-mail armor, their plate armor being restricted to helmet, breast, and shins. But the increasing effectiveness of infantry missile weapons in Europe after the Crusades led the chivalry to rely ever more greatly on plate armor for maximum protection until, by the fifteenth century, it predominated. One weapon that accelerated the trend to greater armor protection for mounted men was the crossbow, the medieval form of the ancient ballista (a crew-served, king-sized bow) but small enough to be operated by a single soldier. The crossbow began to come into prominence as early as the last decades of the eleventh century, and was more and more widely used as the Middle Ages wore on. The bolt, or quarrel, of the crossbow could penetrate chain mail at fifty yards or less and was dangerous to unarmored men to about twice that distance. Made with an iron bow and with a stock for steadying the weapon under the armpit, the crossbow was cocked with either a foot stirrup or a windlass. The pressure of the feudal nobility caused the church's Second Lateran council (1139) to lay a prohibition on the use of crossbows between Christian opponents, though the ban was not uni-formly observed. The greatest technical weakness of the crossbow was its slow rate of fire, no more than two bolts a minute. While performing the relatively lengthy loading procedure, the crossbowman had to be protected by fortifications or other kinds of troops. The most distinguished victim of a crossbow was perhaps Richard I; the English king was mortally wounded by a quarrel during a siege in France in 1199.

An even more remarkable infantry missile weapon of the Middle Ages was the longbow of the English yeomanry, a class of peasant freeholders. Originally a hunting weapon, the longbow's remarkable military potential was discovered by the middle of the thirteenth century, and by the end of King Edward I's reign (1272–1307), archers armed with the weapon com-posed the majority of infantry raised by the English. Six feet in length, its efficient operation required an archer unusually tall and strong for the Middle Ages. The bow was made of elm, hazel, basil or, best of all, yew, and when exercised by skilled hands, it could hurl its "broadcloth" arrow ("broadcloth" was a unit of measurement equal to thirty-seven inches) up to three hundred yards. Even knights in plate armor were vulnerable to the arrows of the longbow at two hundred yards or less, the arrows passing through weak places in the armor and joints. An archer with the longbow could discharge up to six arrows a minute, but, like the crossbowman, he was vulnerable to lance and sword if the enemy could get close enough to use them. Like crossbowmen, archers with the longbow required the pro-tection of other troops or fortifications.

The only infantry armed with pole arms (e.g., pike and halberd) in the Middle Ages who consistently held their own against armored cavalry were the Swiss, primarily because of a discipline and drill unknown to other infantry of the age. A mountainous country inhabited mostly by herdsmen, Switzerland never developed a strong indigenous feudal nobility. Instead it relied on citizen-militia armed with the pike and halberd. In the fourteenth century, the rebelling Swiss cantons overthrew the rule of the dukes of Austria and with their citizen-infantry successfully defended Switzerland from invasion thereafter. On defense, a phalanx of Swiss pike could keep cavalry at bay, and on offense it could sweep through opposing infantry. The pike was supplemented by the axe-like halberd, which could cleave through armor and flesh alike, and, for missile weapons, the Swiss relied on crossbows. The basic Swiss unit was a company of about three hundred men, of which about 250 were pikemen arrayed in a square of sixteen ranks and sixteen files; the remaining men were halberdiers or crossbowmen. The Swiss soldier was protected by a helmet and sometimes a breastplate, but for the most part he relied on the collective strength of the square for his personal protection. The excellence of the Swiss infantry was such that by the fifteenth century other armies were seeking to hire them as mercenaries.

### VI. The Mongol Conquests and Medieval Russia

The most powerful military force of the thirteenth century was not Christian, Turk, or Saracen but the Mongol Golden Horde, which first conquered northern China and Korea and then spread across Siberia to invade Persia and Europe as far as Poland and Hungary. The organizer and original leader of this formidable military machine was Temuchin, who in 1206 took the title of *Ghenghis Khan* ("Mightiest King"). By 1211 he had united the Mongol tribes under his leadership; by 1216 he had completed his Chinese and Korean conquests; and the next year he commenced his advance against the Near East. By the end of 1221 Ghenghis Khan and crushed the Khwarisimian empire in Persia. An army of 20,000 Mongols under his generals Subotai and Jabei then invaded Russia, but was turned back at the Battle of the Kalma river in 1223 by a combined army of Russians and Asian nomads. Ghenghis Khan died in 1227 before he could avenge this defeat, but he had already created the largest contiguous land empire ever seen.

Ogotai, Ghengis Khan's heir, prepared a more systematic conquest of Russia, and in 1237 a Mongol army led by Batu, grandson of Ghengis, swept down on the city of Riazan and then proceeded methodically to destroy cities, towns, and villages throughout northeast Russia. Another Mongol army under Subotai extended the Mongol conquest to southwest Russia, conquering Kiev in December 1237. Adding to Russian difficulties were the near simultaneous attacks from the west by the Swedes and the Teutonic knights. Prince Alexander Nevsky (named for his victory over the Swedes in the battle of the Neva river in 1240) managed to repel the western assaults on Novgorod and Pskov, but the Russian princes were finally compelled to render tribute to the Golden Horde and submit to Mongol dictation. The Mongols permitted the Russians to practice their Eastern, or Orthodox, Christianity, but for more than two centuries the Russians were not masters in their own house.

The subsequent Mongol conquests under Batu and Subotai extended to Poland and even to Hungary, the latter after 120,000 Mongols under Subotai crushed a Hungarian army of 90,000 men under King Bela IV at the Battle of the Sajo river in April 1241. Allegedly, 70,000 of Bela's men were slaughtered, and another 10,000 Hungarians lost their lives when the Mongols sacked Pest. But the death of Ogotai forced Subotai and Batu to suspend their westward drive in order to return to Karakorum to select a new khan. The last great Mongol offensive was directed at the Near East after the middle of the thirteenth century.

A Mongol army under Hulagu, a grandson of Ghenghis Khan, crushed a Turkish army at Baghdad, overran Iraq and Syria, and even penetrated deep into Palestine, but when Hulagu learned that Mangu, the Great Khan and his brother, had died, he and his army began a retirement to the east. In September 1260, a Mameluke army from Egypt caught up with the Mongol rear guard near the Sea of Galilee and cut it to pieces at the Battle of Ain Julut. Ain Julut was the first and only Mongol defeat ever suffered in the Near East. Soon after the Mongol empire in Central Asia began to split into separate khanates, and the great days of Mongol conquest were over.

The power of the Golden Horde has sometimes been attributed to sheer numbers and sometimes to its excellent mounted bowmen. Though certainly numerous, the Mongols never assembled more than 240,000 men for a single campaign (that of Ghenghis Khan against Persia), and individual Mongol armies never exceeded 120,000 men. The real secret of the Mongols' success was excellent discipline, a relatively complex military organization based on the *tumen*, or division of 10,000 men, and sound tactics based on mobile horsemen. The Mongol archers were indeed first-rate, using a powerful bow from the saddle. But whereas sixty percent of the warriors were so armed, a significant forty percent were armored, mounted lancers prepared for shock action. When the two kinds of mounted, missile-shock troops were combined under talented leaders, it is not surprising that they were often superior to any Russian, Near Eastern, or Western military organization of the age.

The great strategic mobility of the Mongols rested on their hearty horses that lived off the country and were relatively impervious to cold and heat but fared better in the grasslands than in forested regions. Mongol soldiers lived off mare's milk and captured cattle, as well as wild game. During their campaigns against the Chinese, the Mongols developed siege weapons out of necessity, and they utilized the catapult and possibly some of the earliest gunpowder siege weapons. After their siege weapons overcame the Chinese fortifications, the relatively primitive works available to the Russians were no match for them. Similarly, the Mongol tactic of mobile envelopment by moving their armies in great crescents, then closing the horns around the flanks of the enemy, often left the less mobile armies of the West confused, cut off from retreat, and demoralized even before the Mongols closed in for a decisive battle.

During the fourteenth century there were so many struggles within the Golden Horde that no fewer than twenty-five khans were pretenders to the throne between 1360 and 1380. When the princes of Moscow exploited Mongol divisions to assert greater independence, a Mongol army was dispatched in 1380 to reassert supremacy. Prince Dimitri Ivanovich's army defeated the Mongols at the Battle of Kulikovo Field (and was thereafter known as Dimitri Domskoy or "Victor of the Don"), but two years later the Mongols compelled Moscow once more to render tribute. Only in 1480, in the reign of Ivan III (1462–1505), also know as Ivan the Great, did Moscovy throw off the "Tatar yoke" and begin to prepare itself to unite much of western Russia under its rule.

## VII. The Hundred Years' War, 1337-1453

### A. The Transformation of War

The last great military drama of the Middle Ages was the Hundred Years' War (1337–1453) between England and France, a war that may be viewed as a transitional phase from the patterns of medieval warfare to those of early modern warfare. Though the war helped to introduce to the West such modern features as gunpowder weapons and semi-permanent royal military forces, at the same time the longbow—a medieval weapon— played a large role in its conduct.

Well before the Hundred Years' War the English had learned in their wars with the Scots that the mere presence of longbows did not guarantee victory. Sound tactics in coordination with other arms were also necessary for the longbow to serve effectively. The point was driven home in 1314, when Edward II's tactical blundering at Bannockburn resulted in a dreadful English defeat at the hands of Scottish knights and *schiltrons* (phalanxes of spearmen). But Edward III demonstrated at Halidon Hill in 1333 that there was a sound tactical system for utilizing the longbow, and in that battle the bow contributed heavily to the defeat of the Scots. The same system, as applied in France during the Hundred Years' War, amounted to taking up a strong defensive position that invited frontal assault, dismounting the knights and using their lances and long stakes carried by the bowmen to shield the archers from the enemy's shock forces and then overwhelming the massed ranks of the enemy with showers of arrows as they advanced.

Though gunpowder was known to the Europeans by at least 1250—and still earlier to the Chinese, Mongols, Turks, and Arabs—it seems to have had little application in the West prior to the Hundred Years' War. One reason may have been that gunpowder—the result of mixing proper proportions of potassium nitrate (saltpeter), sulphur, and charcoal—was difficult to harness for traditional military purposes. In the Hundred Years' War, the first successful application was in bombards, primitive siege guns mentioned as used by the English as early as the siege of Calais (1346–1347). The prototype bombard was essentially a "barrel" or tube of wood or metal reinforced with iron rings, closed at one end (except for a small touch hole), and loaded at the other (the muzzle). The bombard had to be operated from a prepared position, usually a wooden crib constructed opposite the target such as a castle or town wall. The gunpowder was set off by placing a slow-match (smoldering hemp) against the touch hole and, because gunpowder was orginally made between shots, the early bombards were fired at the leisurely rate of one round per hour.

Later bombards made of wrought iron had bores more than two feet in diameter and fired balls so large that they had to be rolled into the muzzles on ramps. The bombard's ammunition consisted of stone balls reinforced with iron hoops, cast iron balls, and, by the early fifteenth century, hollowed-out balls stuffed with pitch for incendiary effect. Bombards were so heavy that they had to be moved on sledges dragged by horses, and their poor mobility made them incapable of keeping up with an army on the march. Accordingly, after a castle or town was placed under siege, days might pass before the bombards arrived, and, even then, thanks to their slow rate of fire, they might require days or even weeks to make a breach in the enemy's walls. Still, given enough time to work its effect, the bombard could bring down the stoutest curtain wall of castle or town.

Next to the bombard, the gunpowder weapon to have the greatest effect in the Hundred Years' War, though mostly near its conclusion, was field artillery made of cast bronze, such as the culverin. Culverins were carried or dragged to earthen mounds or ramparts from where they could fire on enemy troops, and, because of their poor mobility, they could hardly be used except in prepared positions. In the so-called Hussite Wars, 1420–1434, the Bohemian followers of the religious rebel John Hus partially solved the problem of mobility for field guns by mounting them on wagons, but the first guns on wheeled carriages designed for the purpose did not appear in Europe until late in the fifteenth century and well after the conclusion of the Hundred Years' War. As for hand-held firearms, "firesticks" are mentioned in medieval manuscripts as early as 1364, but such firearms remained mostly curiosities until practical types were invented in the sixteenth century.

At the outbreak of the Hundred Years' War, the King of France relied primarily on feudal cavalry, supplemented by mercenary specialists, such as the Genoese crossbowmen, and crudely-armed peasant infantry. With fifteen million French subjects to five million subjects in the Anglo-French empire, and the French chivalry numerically superior to the English knighthood in proportion, the French king had, superficially, a great advantage. But by the time of the Hundred Years' War, the English kings not only had the longbow, they no longer relied primarily on the feudal array. Instead, they raised most of their forces by indenture, or a contract, between the king and experienced captains who obligated themselves, in return for specified sums of money, to supply armed men for stated periods of service. Though such soldiers did not represent a standing or permanent army—indentured troops rarely served longer than a season's campaign at a time—they represented a more permanent, and usually better trained and equipped force than the feudal array which might come together only a few days before a battle.

The chief problem with indentured troops was money, for they were inherently more costly than men serving out of feudal obligation. But their advantages were such that gradually it became clear that even semi-permanent soldiers were a better bargain for monarchs than feudal knights and their retainers if enough money could be found to hire them. And though complete standing or permanent royal armies were in the future, toward the end of the Hundred Years' War the French king took a great step in their direction by founding several companies of ordinance.

## B. 1337–1389: Sluys, Crecy, and Poitiers

The Hundred Years' War commenced when, in 1337, Philip VI of France declared forfeit the territories of Edward III of England in France and attempted to seize them. Edward III not only came to the defense of his French territories, in 1340 he laid claim to the French throne. In the same year, Philip replied to Edward's presumption by assembling two hundred ships, including twenty-four galleys, at the port of Sluys on the Flemmish coast in order to carry an army of invasion to England.

But Philip's naval preparations were known to Edward, and he met the threat by converting 147 English cogs into warships. The cog was a kind of crude sailing ship with a single mast, main sail, and rudimentary rudder and was used for carrying cargo in peacetime. It could be turned into a crude warship, however, by building wooden "castles" on stern and bow in order to shelter archers, and men-at-arms could be stationed in the cog's open "waist." And, rather than risk missing the French fleet after it set forth Edward gambled on a preemptive strike. In June 1340 his fleet suddenly appeared at Sluys, caught the French fleet before many of its soldiers had embarked, and in a day of fighting destroyed or captured all but thirty of Philip's ships. The French never mounted another serious invasion threat to England during the Hundred Years' War.

The first great English victory on land with the longbow came when Edward III's 2,500 men at arms and 7,000 archers faced 30,000 French troops at the battle of Crecy in western France in August 1346. Edward's defensive position was almost perfect for English tactics: rising ground facing a valley in which the French were assembling, the flanks of the English position protected on the one hand by a river and on the other by a woods. The

French advanced their Genoese crossbowmen to soften up the opposition, but they were riddled by longbow arrows before they could get within range of the English line. When the French men-at-arms and infantry charged the English line, the longbow inflicted such a terrible toll that relatively few French survived to reach the English position; those who did survive the rain of arrows were either fended off or killed by the dismounted English men-at-arms. When the French army finally retreated, it left some 1,500 of its chivalry and 10,000 of its other soldiers dead or mortally wounded on the field. Edward's losses probably came to no more than two hundred men.

In the aftermath of Crecy, Edward's army laid siege to Calais, but hostilities were virtually suspended soon after its capture in 1347. Bubonic plague, the terrible Black Death, infected both England and France between 1348 and 1350, and both countries were hit hard. Perhaps a fourth of the French population and a third of the English population died of the disease. The loss of life was so severe that land was abandoned for lack of labor to work it, rents fell off, and taxes went unpaid. In the face of this disaster, it is remarkable that as early as 1355 England and France were again attempting to undertake major military operations against each other.

Fortune continued to go against the French as Edward the Black Prince (so-called for his dark armor) repeated the victory at Crecy at Poitiers in 1356, where 3,600 English men-at-arms and 2,000 archers defeated the attacks of a large French array and captured John II, by then King of France. Eventually, in 1361, the Dauphin (the heir to the French throne) signed the Treaty of Bretigny, yielding to Edward III territory amounting to about a third of France. But the Dauphin (after 1364, Charles V of France) systematically prepared to renew the war with Edward III. He began hiring indentured soldiers, some 6,000 men-at-arms and eight hundred archers by 1368, and he appointed Bertrand du Guesclin—a former *routier* or professional soldier—as Constable of France (commander in chief).

When the war resumed, Guesclin shrewdly avoided the kind of set-piece battles in which the longbow was at its most effective, and instead he caused the French to set ambushes to surprise English columns on the march and to mount surprise attacks on English camps at night. Under this harassment, the English were increasingly forced to shelter in fortified towns and castles, but even in such places they were not secure. The French captured Poitiers and La Rochelle in 1372 and threatened to capture English strongholds in Brittany and Normandy in 1373. The English cause was further damaged when the Black Prince (1376) and Edward III (1377) died of natural causes. Richard II, Edward III's heir, was plagued with internal problems, and his willingness to make peace by giving up Maine in 1389 added to his unpopularity in England. Richard II was eventually deposed by Henry Bolingbroke, Duke of Lancaster, who took the title Henry IV. Upon his death in 1413, his son, the twenty-five-year-old Henry V, ascended the English throne.

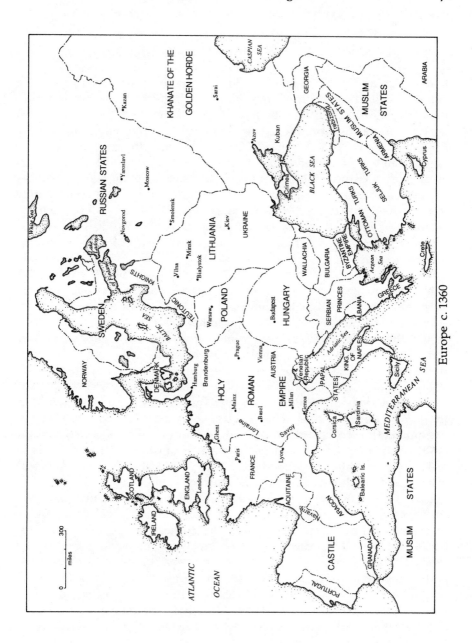

Europe c. 1360

## C. The Final Phase and the Companies of Ordinance

Henry V resumed the war against France in 1415 with no less an ambition than becoming king of England and France, and he came close to achieving his objective. At the battle of Agincourt (1415), the longbow took a terrible toll of the Constable d'Albret's forces as he committed the same kind of tactical blunder that the French commanders had committed against the English at Crecy and Poitiers. D'Albret's life and those of 10,000 other Frenchmen were forfeited in the bargain. But Agincourt was to be the last great English victory with the longbow on French soil. Though in the wake of Agincourt and subsequent English victories, the Duke of Burgundy threw in with the English in 1416, and in 1420 Charles VI disowned the Dauphin's continued resistance and recognized Henry V as his heir, the war was still not ended when both Henry V and Charles VI died of natural causes in 1422.

Henry VI being a minor, an English regency continued the war in his name, but in 1429 Joan of Arc, an illiterate seventeen-year-old girl from Lorraine, convinced the Dauphin that God had chosen her to be the instrument of French salvation. He allowed her to accompany an army trying to raise the English siege of Orleans, and the subsequent victory so inspired the French that they seized several fortified places from the English. Accompanied by the "Maid of Orleans," the French army finally marched to Rheims where the Dauphin was consecrated as Charles VII of France. Though Joan was subsequently betrayed into enemy hands and burned at the stake at Rouen in 1430, the religious nationalism she had helped stimulate among the French did not die with her. In 1435 the Duke of Burgundy deserted the English and switched to the side of Charles VII; in 1436 Paris was recaptured after a fourteen-year occupation; and in 1444 the nearly exhausted English consented to the Truce of Tours.

The Truce of Tours left much of France still in English hands, and over the next five years Charles VII laid the foundations of a royal army capable of expelling the English altogether. The cornerstone of this army was twenty companies of ordinance, each company a unit of about six hundred mounted men paid on a regular basis for a year at a time, each equipped and organized according to royal specifications (hence, "of ordinance"), and all mounted. The captain, two lieutenants and an ensign—the company's commissioned officers—were chosen by the monarch and served at his pleasure, and although the *gendarmerie*, the armored lancers among the company, provided mounted shock-troops, they were trained to fight on foot as well. The other members of the company were equipped with spears and swords and normally fought on foot. The regular pay enjoyed by the companies of ordinance insured that their spare time was spent in training rather than in seeking the means of survival. Charles VII also enlisted a corps of *franc-archers*—8,000 selected bowmen—for extended service. Finally, Charles ordered Jean Bureau, a master gunner, to assemble bombards and other guns for a royal artillery train. When the Hundred Years' War resumed in the summer of 1449, Charles VII's army of 30,000 men was a formidable force, two-thirds of which were in his pay.

Commanded by the Constable Richemont, the French army demonstrated its new strength by quickly capturing Rouen, the capital of Normandy, and then—Bureau's bombards playing a starring role in bringing down walls around such places—capturing Harfleur and adjacent towns during the winter of 1449–1450. By the spring of 1450 the French had completed their conquest of Normandy save Caen, the Cherbourg peninsula, and Bayeux. In April an English army of 4,000 troops commanded by Sir Thomas Kyriell tried to come to the aid of Bayeux, then besieged by the French, and near the village of Formigny occupied a classic English defensive position where it awaited a French frontal attack. Instead of obliging the English, the French brought up two culverins and began systematically pelting the ranks of the English beyond the range of the longbow. The enraged English bowmen rushed forward to seize the guns only to find that they had been drawn into a trap. French cavalry rode them down before the English knights could come to their aid, and, in the general melee that followed, the English were so throughly beaten that Kyriell was taken prisoner and 3,774 of his men were killed or seriously wounded. The English had not been so disastrously defeated in the field since Bannockburn (1314).

After their defeat at Formigny, the English lost Bayeux and, in succession, their remaining bastions in Normandy until the last—Cherbourg—surrendered in August 1450. Between 1450 and 1453 the English strongholds in Guyenne went the same way. The final English effort to turn the tide occurred during the French siege of Castillon, near Bordeaux, in July 1453. On that occasion, the Earl of Shrewsbury led 6,000 troops in a frontal assault on a French earthen rampart studded with culverins. The consequence was that the culverins slaughtered the English with powder and ball in much the same way that longbow arrows had once slaughtered rash French charges at Crecy, Poitiers, and Agincourt. The French went on to take Castillon, and, when Bordeaux fell to them the following October, the Hundred Years' War came to an end. Of a once extensive English empire in France, only Calais survived. More important for this study, by the close of the Hundred Years' War new patterns of war were emerging in the West.

# FOUR

# Early Modern Land Warfare, 1494–1721

## I. The Wars for Italy, 1494–1559

### A. The Debut of the Early Modern Army

At the conclusion of the Hundred Years' War in 1453, Charles VII of France retained a few companies of ordinance in order to possess a force with which he could maintain internal order and as a foundation for an expanded royal army in wartime. Eventually, the companies of ordinance were transformed into squadrons of gendarmerie (heavy cavalry), to which, in 1479, Louis XI (r. 1461–1483) added companies of Swiss mercenaries armed with pike and halberd. In the reign of Charles VIII (1483–1498), the proportion of infantry in the French army was increased to two-thirds of its 30,000 men, but Charles's chief contribution was his modernization of French artillery. His guns, both siege and field, were the first mounted on wheeled carriages drawn by horses, and mobile enough to keep up with the army on the march. They could go into action without lengthy delays and possessed a greater rate of fire than the old-style bombards and culverins. They were, in fact, the prototypes of the smoothbore, muzzle-loading guns used by European armies well into the nineteenth century.

The Wars for Italy (1494–1559), the first of the early modern wars, commenced in the spring of 1494 when Charles VIII personally led his army across the Alps and invaded the Italian city-states. European observers were stunned by the speed with which his army systematically smashed all opposition in its path. When the *condottieri* (armies under a *condotta*, or contract, to the Italian city-states and mostly equipped as men-in-arms) avoided battle in the field by retiring behind the walls of castles and towns that could have resisted the old bombards for weeks, the new French guns breached them in a matter of hours. The campaign reached its climax in February 1495 when Charles's army forced the surrender of Naples. After detaching a garrison under the Duke of Nemours to hold southern Italy, Charles's army commenced a return march to France, and, while passing through northern Italy in July, nearly wiped out an army of condottieri near Fornovo. At least symbolically, the Battle of Fornovo laid to rest the medieval military tradition.

By the time Charles concluded his campaign, acute Italian observers such as Niccolo Machiavelli (1469–1527)—the sometime Florentine diplomat, political scientist, and military commentator—grasped that the future lay with the large, centralized royal state such as France and that unless Italy quickly presented a united front to the outside world, it would be the prey of foreign powers. The new politics and warfare are reflected in Machiavelli's *The Prince* and *Art of War*, both intended as guides to the Italian prince who would save his country by uniting it by whatever means were necessary. Unfortunately for Italy, a united Italian nation-state would not appear for three and a half centuries after Machiavelli's death, and, in the meantime (and as Machiavelli predicted), Italy was frequently the objective and battleground for powers more united and powerful than itself.

### B. The Spanish Army to 1559

Charles VIII's campaign in Italy caused Milan, Venice, the Pope, the Holy Roman emperor, and the Kingdom of Spain (united in the persons of King Ferdinand of Aragon and Queen Isabella of Castile) to ally themselves against France. The members of the coalition against France changed from time to time in a conflict that lasted, off and on, sixty-five years, but Spain finally proved to be the most formidable French rival. Even so, the development of the early modern Spanish army was not accomplished without setbacks.

Europe c. 1560

In its struggle to expel the Moors from Spain during the fifteenth century, the Spanish army was composed of genitors (i.e., light cavalry), infantry armed with sword and buckler (the buckler was a small shield), and town militia armed with pike. A combination of these forces had driven the Moors from Granada, their last foothold in Spain, in 1492, but the experience gave the Spanish an exaggerated self-confidence. In 1495 the Spanish army entered southern Italy to expel the French, only to suffer a heavy defeat at the Battle of Seminara at the hands of the Duke of Nemours. Following its defeat, the Spanish army was modernized by strengthening its heavy cavalry, hiring *Landsknechten* (German mercenaries who, like the Swiss, were armed with pike and halberd), and, most important, by adding companies of infantry equipped with the arquebus and the musket, the first reasonably efficient infantry firearms used in large numbers.

The Spanish arquebus was a muzzle-loading, smoothbore matchlock that was four feet in length, weighed nine pounds, and fired a lead ball weighing less than an ounce. The Spanish musket, adopted a few years after the arquebus, was also a matchlock and a smoothbore, but was six feet in length and weighed about twenty pounds. It was a crew-served weapon that fired a two-ounce lead ball and had a barrrel so heavy that it required a rest for

Soldier Loading Matchlock Musket.
William Reid, *Weapons Through the Ages* (New York: Crescent Books, 1986 ed.), p. 101.

firing. Both arquebus and musket were muzzle-loading, and each was primed by adding a dash of gunpowder to the pan at the base of the barrel. The piece was discharged by pressing a trigger that caused a serpentine, holding a smoldering piece of hemp, to rotate into the pan. The resulting flash in the pan sent flame through the touch hole into the barrel, igniting the main charge. Both the arquebus and musket required about a minute to reload, and accuracy was so poor that the typical marksman could not reliably hit a man-sized target at ranges above seventy-five yards. Moreover, arquebusiers and musketeers had to be protected by pikemen or earthworks on the battlefield. Still, the arquebus and musket could penetrate any practical thickness of body armor, and they made infantry firepower an increasingly important factor in battle.

Hernandez Gonzalo de Cordoba ("El Gran Capitan"), Ferdinand's finest general, avenged his defeat at Seminara by taking the measure of the French under the Duke of Nemours at the Battle of Cerignola in April 1503. He had his army take up a defensive position on a hill, his pikemen and swordsmen defending earthworks at its base and his arquebusiers deployed higher up the slope where they could fire over his troops in the front line. The Duke of Nemours was so arrogant that he did not even bother to deploy his artillery before leading his infantry and cavalry forward in a frontal attack on the Spanish position. When the Spanish pike and swordsmen contained the French assault at the earthworks, the arquebusiers on the hillside above them poured such a withering fire into the French ranks that the Duke of Nemours was only one among the numerous French killed by the Spanish bullets. Gonzalo completed his victory by launching a counterattack with infantry and cavalry that swept the remains of the shattered French army from the field. In the wake of the Battle of Cerignola, the Spanish army occupied Naples, defeated the French again in December at the Battle of the Garigliano river, and finally drove them into northern Italy.

The Spanish army continued to evolve in modern directions more rapidly than the French. Around 1505 the Spanish introduced the colonelcy, the forerunner of the modern battalion, which amounted to a temporary grouping of four or five companies of infantry on the battlefield under a officer designated as a *coronel* (colonel). The pikemen of the companies formed a square and arquebusiers massed on its flanks in formations as deep as sixteen ranks. The arquebusier at the head of each file fired his weapon, then went to the rear of the file and reloaded while working his way to the head of the file again. Constant motion in the ranks made simultaneous firing by volley impossible, but the short range of the firearms, the time-consuming motions of reloading, and the need to protect arquebusiers and musketeers with pikemen left no other choice. (Indeed, the problem of combining fire and shock in the same formation would not be entirely solved until the combining of the flintlock musket and the socket bayonet two centuries later.)

The Spanish also developed an administrative grouping of companies called the *tercio*, the forerunner of the "regiment," a term the French introduced later. The tercio was commanded by a colonel assisted by a lieutenant-colonel, and, in 1534, was standardized at about 3,000 men, twelve companies, and 250 men to a company. A commissioned officer known as a major headed a small staff which assisted the colonel with his administrative chores. Responsiblity for the training of the soldiers and for forming the Spanish army for battle, was exercised by the sergeant-major-general, usually an old veteran who had come up through the ranks and who was assisted in his duties by the sergeant-major of each tercio and the sergeants and corporals of the companies, the non-commissioned officers. In varying forms, the Spanish organization was eventually adopted by other armies, and, in the next century, the sergeant-major-general was replaced by the major-general, a commissioned officer only second in rank to the commander of a field army, who, unless the king himself, usually bore the rank of captain-general, lieutenant-general, colonel-general, constable, or marshal.

Despite the Spanish advantages, the struggle between the Spanish and French for control of northern Italy was long and hard. In 1512 the Spanish suffered a defeat at the battle of Ravenna that may have led them to abandon the sword and buckler in favor of equipping their infantry entirely with pikes or firearms, two pikemen for every arquebusier or musketeer. The increased Spanish firepower produced by this reform may have been responsible for the Spanish victory at La Motta in 1513, though in the same year it was Spanish "push of pike" that settled the outcome at the Battle of Novara. In the hard fought Battle of Marignano in 1515, the French used artillery to smash the Spanish squares so that cavalry could successfully charge them, but the Spanish countered this tactic by increasingly taking position behind field works that gave them some protection against artillery fire. The combination of such breastworks and infantry fire gave the Spanish a victory at the Battle of La Bicocca in 1522 when, at its conclusion, some 3,000 enemy Swiss pikemen lay dead before the Spanish lines. After La Bicocca the French too began to rely more on defensive field works, but the tables were turned at the Battle of Pavia in 1525. The Spanish infantry surprised the French by outflanking their entrenchments, and, by forcing them to make a counterattack, exposed them to annihilating infantry fire.

Thanks to dynastic developments in these years, the strategic as well as the tactical situation darkened for France. In 1516 Charles Habsburg inherited the Spanish throne from his maternal grandfather Ferdinand, and in 1519 he succeeded his paternal grandfather, Maximilian I, as Holy Roman emperor. As King Charles I Spain and Holy Roman Emperor Charles V, he was probably the most powerful European monarch up to his time since Charlemagne. Moreover, thanks to the Spanish voyages of discovery around the globe in the late fifteenth and early sixteenth centuries (see next chapter), Charles ruled a vast overseas empire that included much of the New World, and its gold and silver helped to finance his army and navy. By the end of Charles V's reign, Habsburg power was firmly ensconced at the Pyrenees, in Italy, and on the Rhine.

The French Valois kings did not accept Charles V's supremacy in Europe without a struggle, and in 1536 Francis I went so far as to make an alliance with Suleiman I ("the Magnificent"), sultan of the Ottoman Turkish Empire. The Turkish armies were already deep in the Balkans, having wiped out the Hungarian army at Mohacs in 1526, subsequently occupied most of Hungary, and threatened Vienna in 1529. Though Charles V's forces managed to turn back the Turkish threat to Austria, the constant Turkish menace from southeastern Europe diverted his resources and attention from the conduct of the war with France.

Charles V's problems were further compounded by the religious revolt led by Martin Luther in Germany. The Lutheran or Protestant cause became a rallying point for German princes eager for an excuse to be politically and religiously independent of the emperor and ultimately precipitated a civil war in the Holy Roman empire. While Charles was preoccupied in trying to suppress the revolt, Henry II of France (r.1547–1559) was able to seize his imperial territories of Metz, Toul, and Verdun and thus advance the French frontier that much nearer the Rhine. When Charles V finally concluded that his measures to stamp out Protestantism in Germany were only leading to the empire's dissolution, he accepted the Peace of Augsburg (1555) which allowed each prince to choose between Catholicism and Lutheranism for his subjects.

Charles retired from the Spanish throne in favor of his son Philip II in 1555, and from the throne of the Holy Roman empire in 1556 in favor of his brother Ferdinand I, thus creating two dynasties, the Spanish Habsburgs and the Austrian Habsburgs. In the division of Charles's empire, Philip II acquired the Netherlands, formerly part of the Holy Roman empire, and used the Low Countries as a base from which to threaten northern France. From that base the Duke of Savoy and 50,000 Spanish troops won such a victory at the Battle of St. Quentin in northern France in 1557 that Henry II was forced to recall troops from Italy. After the French were beaten again in 1558 at the Battle of Gravelines, Henry II ended the Wars for Italy by signing the compromise Peace of Cateau Cambrésis in 1559. Under its terms, France retained Metz, Toul, and Verdun, and, on the coast, Calais (taken from the English in 1558) but gave up its claims to Italy. Spain replaced France as the dominant power in the Italian peninsula and as the greatest military power in Europe.

## II. The Dutch Revolt, 1568–1648

### A. The Eighty Years' War

In 1568 Philip II's centralizing policies and intolerance of the spread of Protestantism to the Netherlands finally triggered a revolt against his rule that became one of longest conflicts in European history, one that finally blended into the wider European struggle known as the Thirty Years' War (1618–1648). In its early stages, Philip's "Army of Flanders" waged a vengeful war of political and religious suppression under a succession of Spanish commanders including the Duke of Alba (or Alva), Luis de Requesens, Don John of Austria (Philip's half brother), and Alessandro Farnese (Duke of Parma). Philip II spared none of his resources in prosecuting war, though conflicts with the Ottoman Turks in the Mediterranean was another preoccupation. At times the size of the Army of Flanders rose as high as 100,000 men, though more typically it numbered about 60,000 men, and the opposition never amounted to more than 30,000 men under arms at one time. In 1595 the army of Maurice of Nassau, the greatest of the Dutch commanders, came to just 10,000 infantry, 2,000 cavalry, and forty-two pieces of artillery.

Nevertheless, the Spanish made only limited progress toward repressing the revolt until, upon the death of Don John in 1578, command in the Netherlands fell to the Duke of Parma. The best of Philip II's generals, Parma waged systematic campaigns that secured one place after another in the southern Netherlands (roughly Belgium today) until his efforts were rewarded by the capture of Antwerp in 1585. Meanwhile, the assassination in 1584 of William the Silent, Prince of Orange and the principal leader of the revolt, inflicted another heavy blow to Philip's enemies.

But Parma's progress was counter-productive in that it alarmed Elizabeth I, the Protestant queen of England, who feared that if Philip II was finally victorious in the Low Countries, he might use the Netherlands as a base of invasion against England. Elizabeth's fears prompted her to sign an alliance with the United Provinces in 1585 and to send troops under the Earl of Leicester to aid in their defense. She also continued her tolerance of unofficial English forays against Spanish shipping and overseas colonies, and, in turn, Philip II secretly plotted Elizabeth's overthrow and the substitution of her Catholic cousin, Mary Queen of Scots, on the English throne. After Mary's execution in February 1587, Philip turned to overt means to overthrow Elizabeth's government, and in the summer of 1588 he sent the "Invincible Armada" to the coast of Flanders in expectation that it would link up with part of Parma's army for an invasion of England. But, as will be discussed in the next chapter, the English and Dutch fleets managed to prevent the junction of the two forces, most of the Armada was subsequently destroyed by battle and storm, and, in consequence, Philip's problems with England and the Dutch went unsolved.

In 1589 Philip II further reduced his chances of victory over the Dutch by ordering Parma to use part of the Army of Flanders to assist the Catholic League in the French War of the Three Henrys, a civil-religious conflict involving Henry Bourbon (champion of the Huguenots or French Calvinists), Henry Guise (leader of the Catholic League), and Henry III (the last king of the Valois line). But both Henry Guise and Henry III were assassinated before Spanish intervention became effective, and in 1589 the Protestant Henry took the French throne as Henry IV and founded the Bourbon dynasty. Parma died in 1592 while campaigning in northern France, and the following year Henry IV reconciled many of his Catholic countrymen to his rule by formally converting to Catholicism. In 1598, the year in which Philip II died, Henry IV issued the Edict of Nantes to protect his Huguenot subjects and formally ended the war with Spain through the Treaty of Vervins.

Philip III (r. 1598–1621) doggedly continued the war against the Dutch until 1609 when his general Ambrogio de Spinola recommended a long armistice in which the Army of Flanders might recover from its manpower and financial difficulties. The Twelve Year Truce (1609–1621) ended in the same year that Philip IV came to the throne, but Spain was too involved in the Thirty Years' War in Germany to send Spinola forces adequate to his needs. The Army of Flanders eventually dwindled to 20,000 men. Finally, as part of the general Peace of Westphalia, which ended the Thirty Years' War in 1648, Spain formally recognized the independence of the United Provinces. Given that the Spanish Habsburgs were to lose even the Spanish Netherlands (i.e., the ten provinces in the south) in the next century, about all the Eighty Years' War did for Spain was to exhaust its treasury and accelerate its decline as a great power.

### B. Patterns in the Eighty Years' War

Spain's inability to crush the rebellion of a people markedly inferior in population (perhaps two million people lived in the Netherlands) and resources compared to those of the Spanish Habsburgs was due to many reasons, including foreign intervention and Philip II's misjudgments and diversions of strength regarding England and France. But the patterns of war in this period made the task exceedingly difficult in any case. One reason was that the Dutch had refortified their towns and cities according to the new techniques of the *trace italienne,* developed after the old-style medieval fortifications in Italy had proven so ineffective against the new French artillery in the Wars for Italy. The *trace italienne* called for building fortifications of very thick earthen walls or ramparts, sometimes faced with brick, and, at intervals along those ramparts, so-call bastions, actually mini-fortresses studded with artillery. The thick ramparts tended to absorb the projectiles of the smoothbore guns, and the bastions provided the fortress with interlocking fields of fire that could shatter infantry assaults on ramparts or bastions. When such fortresses were also surrounded by flooded or boggy terrain, as was nearly always the case in the Dutch Netherlands, they were almost impossible to take by direct assault. Spanish offensives in the Low Countries repeatedly bogged down in the most literal sense of the term.

Another reason for the Spanish failure was logistical in nature. The sea route from Spain to the Netherlands could be traversed by sailing ships within two weeks but was too insecure for Spain to rely on it to meet the needs of the Army of Flanders for either supplies or reinforcements. Beyond needs that could be met locally, or from neighboring German states, the Army of Flanders was dependent on the Spanish road, the southern terminus of which lay in northern Italy. It was customary for Spanish troops bound for the Low Countries to assemble in northern Italy, commence a march through passes in the western Alps to the Franche-Comté and Lorraine (both now in eastern France), and complete their trip to the Low Countries by marching through the Ardennes. The route was so primitive in the sixteenth century that over some stretches only pack animals could accompany the troops and as many as two months might be consumed on the way.

A third reason for Spain's failure involved state bankruptcies. The flow of wealth from Spain's overseas empire was not inexhaustible, and far too little of it that arrived was invested in economic enterprises that might have matured for Spain's benefit and made it strong for the long term. The constant squandering of overseas wealth in war meant that Spain had to borrow heavily, and often the wealth in gold and silver arriving from the New World was pledged in advance to repay loans. Moreover, delays in pay often incited revolts among the mercenary soldiers in the Army of Flanders, most of whom were not Spanish and for whom the war in the Netherlands was an occupation, not a cause.

A final factor in the Spanish defeat was the leadership demonstrated by Maurice of Nassau, the second son of William the Silent, who was appointed admiral-general of the Netherlands and captain-general of troops of Brabant and Flanders in 1589. He managed to turn a motley collection of mercenary and native soldiers into a formidable army through drill and discipline, and, though the Dutch army was a small one by Spanish standards, Maurice multiplied its effectiveness by reducing the size of Dutch battalions to 520 men, arming half of each battalion with firearms and thus endowing his units with more flexibility and firepower on the battlefield than the larger but clumsier Spanish formations. Maurice also tried to avoid the kind of formal battles in the field that favored the Spanish, and during twenty years of command, he fought only two such actions—Tournhout in 1597 and Nieuport in 1600. He preferred his army to attack exposed enemy outposts, fortresses, and supply columns and was the first modern general to follow the Roman practice of requiring every soldier to include a spade in his equipment. During his career his army recaptured at least twenty-nine Spanish-held forts and fortresses and forced the Spanish to abandon at least three sieges. Maurice practiced a strategy that, in contemporary parlance, might be called protracted warfare, one that aimed at exhausting the patience and treasury of the King of Spain rather than seeking the annihilation of his forces. Such a strategy was suitable to the spirit of the Dutch, the technology of the time, the geography and topography of the arena of war, and the Dutch religious and political goals. When its effects were reinforced by Spanish misjudgments and diversions of strength elsewhere, it proved ultimately successful.

## III. The Thirty Years' War, 1618–1648

### A. The Reforms of Gustavus Adolphus

The religious Peace of Augsburg (1555) maintained a precarious settlement in the Holy Roman empire until early in the seventeenth century when the imperial authorities became increasingly concerned that Calvinism—a particularly virulent strain of Protestantism forbidden under the Peace of Augsburg—was spreading to certain states of the empire. A Calvinist rebellion in Bohemia in 1618 led to Imperial repression in 1620 and to a war between Catholics and Protestants across Germany. Denmark intervened on the side of the German Protestant states in 1626, but by 1629 Imperial forces had defeated the Danes and carried the Imperial flag to the southern shores of the Baltic Sea. Lacking an Austrian Habsburg army *per se*, Emperor Ferdinand II depended in these years on princes of the empire—such as Elector Maximilian of Bavaria and Albrecht Wallenstein, Duke of Friedland and Mecklenburg—to raise troops for him, and on Spanish troops provided by Philip IV, his royal cousin.

The tide of the war swung in favor of the anti-Imperials when, in 1630, Protestant King Gustavus Adolphus of Sweden landed at Peenemunde at the head of an army of 40,000 men and set about liberating the German Baltic provinces. Sweden's royal army was unusual for its day in that it was composed almost entirely of men of one nationality, its soldiers pressed under a universal military service law. This homogenous character did not last long, however, for Gustavus was compelled to leave part of his army to protect Sweden, and his losses in Germany forced him to employ many foreign mercenaries to maintain his army's strength. Even so, he avoided the usual custom of hiring mercenaries by whole companies and instead integrated them as individuals in existing units, in a sense inventing the modern private soldier. His measure helped to develop and maintain unit *esprit de corps* peculiar to permanent military organizations with established traditions. Moreover, Gustavus was an ardent disciple of Maurice of Nassau, adopting and improving on many of his military reforms, including smaller and more flexible infantry battalions and the practice of musket firing in volleys.

The infantry regiments of the Swedish army normally consisted of eight companies of 150 men each. On the battlefield, each regiment divided into two battalions of six hundred men each, each battalion in nine ranks, the first six equipped with muskets, the last three with pikes. The Swedish musket was an improved matchlock that did not require a barrel rest, was five feet in length, and weighed about ten pounds. The musketeers were also equipped with paper cartridges (pre-measured powder and ball in paper packages) which facilitated faster loading than the old way of keeping powder, ball, and patch in separate containers. The first three ranks in each infantry company fired a simultaneous volley, then interchanged with the musketeers behind in order to reload while they fired. The Swedes became so skilled at this maneuver that their infantry battalions could discharge two volleys per minute. Gustavus also added two small guns— called four-pounders after the weight of their solid shot—to each of his regiments, the guns to be manhandled about the battlefield in order to keep up with the maneuvers of the infantry battalions and to add to their firepower. Heavier guns, as in other armies, had to remain stationary during battle, but Gustavus's pieces were exceptionally well-served by crews trained under artillery officers.

Gustavus also reformed the Swedish cavalry, abolishing the widely used tactic of the *caracole* (successive waves of riders approaching the enemy infantry in order to fire their matchlock pistols, then filing to the rear) in favor of arming his cavalry with the saber and committing them against infantry when shock action seemed likely to succeed. He created the first dragoons, or mounted troops armed with the carbine (a short musket) and a wheel lock pistol which achieved ignition with a spring-actuated grinding wheel that dropped sparks into the pan. The dragoons usually fought dismounted in order to seize and hold positions in advance of the rest of the army, but they were later armed with the saber and could fight from the saddle.

### B. Gustavus vs. Wallenstein

After Sweden intervened in the Thirty Years' War, the fate of northern Germany was sealed when Gustavus's army defeated an Imperial army of 36,000 troops commanded by Count Johann Tilly at the Battle of Breitenfeld in September 1631. The number and rate of fire of Gustavus's artillery (seventy-five Swedish guns to twenty-six Imperial guns), the rapid volleys of the Swedish infantry battalions, and the shock-action of the well-timed Swedish cavalry charges stunned the Imperial forces and forced their retreat. Gustavus's army followed its beaten foe into southern Germany, liberated the Palatinate (whose elector Frederick II had been briefly the protestant king of Bohemia between 1619 and 1620), and in the spring of 1632 defeated Tilly's army a second time at the battle of Rain on the river Lech. Tilly died of his wounds a few weeks later. The Swedish army went on to occupy many places in Bavaria, while the forces of the Elector of Saxony, Gustavus's ally, occupied parts of Bohemia.

In the crisis for the Imperial cause created by Gustavus's victories, the emperor called on Wallenstein to raise a new army. In the summer of 1632 Wallenstein's forces skillfully maneuvered the Saxons out of Bohemia and

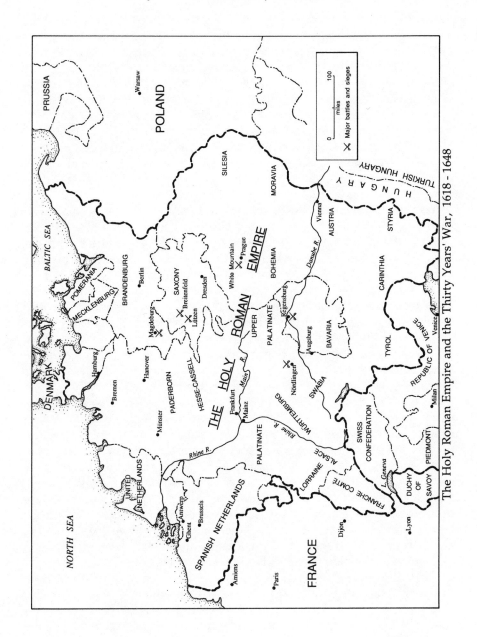

The Holy Roman Empire and the Thirty Years' War, 1618 - 1648

managed to link up with Elector Maximilian's forces holding Regensburg in Bavaria. Wallenstein was aided by the fact that Gustavus's army, then near Nuremberg, was experiencing increasing difficulty in feeding itself from local resources, and he correctly anticipated that Gustavus would either have to abandon his position or risk a quick offensive to destroy Wallenstein's army. Accordingly, Wallenstein had his army fortify a strong position near the ruins of an old castle called Alte Veste (or Alte Feste) southwest of Fuerth and there awaited Gustavus's attack. Gustavus did not fail to deliver it, and in a two-day battle in Septmeber, he launched repeated assaults on Wallenstein's field works only to lose perhaps as many 7,000 men to no purpose. The battle of Alte Veste was Gustavus's first serious reverse in the campaign.

After the battle of Alte Veste, the opposing armies tried to outmaneuver each other and find enough supplies to live on at the same time. By November 1632, the strength of Gustavus's army had been reduce by hunger, disease, and battle to 18,000 men as it waited in an entrenched position near Naumburg. Wallenstein had abandoned operations for the winter, distributing his 30,000 troops among winter camps around Leipzig, the most important concentration being at Luetzen. Though prudence dictated that Gustavus remain on the defensive until he received reinforcements and supplies, when he learned that part of the Imperial army at Leutzen had been detailed off under Count Johann von Pappenheim to seek food, he threw caution to the winds and ordered his army to take the offensive in hopes of defeating Wallenstein's forces while divided.

Gustavus's sudden winter offensive surprised Wallenstein, who barely had time to send word to Pappenhem to return with his detachment, but he managed to gather 20,000 men to confront the oncoming enemy. As the battle on November 16 was beginning, Gustavus was killed in a skirmish, and Prince Bernhard of Saxe-Weimar had to assume command of his forces. Despite the loss of Gustavus, Bernhard's army managed to win a hard-fought battle, finally inflicting 12,000 casualties on the Imperials, capturing their artillery and forcing them to retreat from the field, but the victory was pyrrhic. Gustavus's former army suffered 10,000 casualties, more than half its strength, and the loss of Gustavus as a commander and inspiration to his men was irreplaceable.

The failure of the Imperial forces to exploit Gustavus's death to their advantage was as much due to Wallenstein's machinations as to military factors. He was distracted by the prospects of a separate peace with Ferdinand II's enemies and their acceptance of him as the independent king of Bohemia. He spent more time in his 1633 campaign in Silesia seeking terms with Brandenburg, Saxony, and Sweden than he did in seeking victories, and when he did almost nothing to stop a revived Swedish-German army under General Gustavus Horn and Bernhard from overrunning Alsace, Franconia, Swabia, and Bavaria, the Emperor's suspicions were confirmed. Matters came to a head in January 1634 when Wallenstein assembled fifty of his generals and colonels at Pilsen in Bohemia and sought their oaths of loyalty in preparation for a mass defection. Before Wallenstein could pursue his treason, Ferdinand II revoked his commission, placed him under an Imperial ban, and ordered his arrest. Wallenstein attempted to flee to the camps of the emperor's enemies, but his own troops murdered him at Eger in February 1634.

### C. The Final Phases

Wallenstein's defection and death damaged the morale of the Imperials, but the arrival of Spanish Habsburg troops helped to revive their hopes for final victory. In July 1634, and while commanded by the Spanish general Cardinal-Infante, the Imperial army repeatedly repelled attacks by Bernhard's and Horn's army at the Battle of Noerdlingen and so damaged their forces that thereafter the Swedish army's military participation in the Thirty Years' War faded. In 1635 France entered the war to become the foremost among the Habsburg enemies, despite the fact that France was largely Catholic. Cardinal Richelieu, Louis XIII's chief minister, was eager to exploit the war for French expansion at the expense of the German emperor, and Cardinal Mazarin followed that policy after the deaths of Richelieu in 1642 and Louis XIII in 1643. Though a regency during the minority of Louis XIV faced serious internal problems, near the end of the Thirty Years' War the French armies were ably led by Marshal Turenne and the Duke of Enghien (later the Prince Condé), and in 1643 the French army enjoyed a crushing victory over the Spanish army at the Battle of Rocroi, the last major action of the war. Peace was restored to Germany in 1648, and when the state of war between France and Spain was officially closed by the Peace of the Pyrenees in 1659, the predominant military power for the next half century was to be Louis XIV's France.

### D. The Impact of the Thirty Years' War

Though historians divide over just how true is the tradition of the "all-consuming fury of the Thirty Years' War," perhaps a quarter of the German population of sixteen million perished as the result of fighting, atrocities, hunger, disease, banditry and other misadventures between 1618 and 1648. The population of Bohemia—perhaps three million people at the beginning of the war—may have been reduced by two-thirds. Over the empire as a whole, towns and villages were wiped out, and even relatively large cities were not spared. Magdeburg, in which 25,000 out of 30,000 people were indiscriminately butchered by Imperial troops in 1631, has been called the "Hiroshima of the Thirty Years' War." In general, the experience of the war was to demonstrate that lack of restraint could be destructive to the interests of all sides and helped to inspire some of the first modern efforts at establishing "international law" governing the conduct of military forces and their treatment of civilians. Probably the most influential writer of the period in this regard was Hugo Grotius (Huigh de Groot) whose *Law of War and Peace* (1625) drew on both ancient Roman law and logic to justify a system of rules for limiting the conduct of war.

Though their goal of a centralized and religiously orthodox German empire was never reached, the Austrian Habsburgs reaped some unexpected benefits from the Thirty Years' War. The military residue of Wallenstein's army—nine regiments of infantry, ten regiments of cavalry, and some artillery units—left them with the foundations of a permanent army. Never again would the emperor be quite so dependent on the support of the princes of the empire for military forces as before 1648. As the Austrian Habsburg army expanded, it proved capable of driving the Turks from Hungary into the Balkans, and thus the Austrian empire—as distinct from the Holy Roman empire—became a new factor in international politics. In addition, the war accelerated the decline in the use of armor by infantry as the trend was increasingly toward more casualties being inflicted by fire weapons than shock weapons. By the middle of the seventeenth century, cavalry had gravitated to so-called half-body armor (open face helmets and protection for arm, torso and upper leg). As armor became less common, the uniform became more important as outer wear.

### IV. The Early Modern Army in England to 1661

#### A. The Anglo-Scottish Wars

After a period of internal disorders in England known as the War of the Roses (1455–1485), Henry VII established the Tudor dynasty, but the only standing or permanent Tudor military forces at the beginning of the modern period were palace guards and fortress garrisons. But England's only potential enemy within Britain was Scotland, a country with a smaller population and fewer resources, and as the greater danger of invasion seemed to be from the continent, both Henry VII and Henry VIII (r. 1513–1547) placed priority on a strong fleet. They assumed that forces needed to cope with a Scottish threat could be created as the need arose and from so-called trained bands of militia and veterans with previous military experience in English or foreign armies.

Scotland too relied mainly on improvised forces in the sixteenth century and was chiefly a military threat to England when in alliance with France. When in 1513 Henry VIII joined forces with the Holy Roman emperor Maximilian I to invade France during the Wars for Italy, James IV of Scotland countered by leading an army of 50,000 men in an invasion of northern England. Thomas Howard, Earl of Surrey, assembled an English army of 25,000 men to repel the threat, and in September he defeated James IV's army at the Battle of Flodden Field, in which James was killed. In what

The English Civil Wars, 1642 - 1651

seemed like an anachronistic replay of a scene from the Hundred Years' War, English longbows shattered the Scottish *schiltrons*, or attacking formations of spearmen, almost as they had slaughtered the formations of attacking French knights at Agincourt almost a century earlier. The sense of anachronism continued almost to the middle of the century when, after war had broken out again between England and Scotland in 1542, the outcome was decided at the Battle of Pinkie in 1547 by opposing bodies of armored cavalry. Pinkie ended in a victory for the English and was the last formal battle between England and Scotland as separate monarchies.

## B. Stuart Policy and the English Civil War

When Elizabeth I, daughter of Henry VIII, died in 1603 unmarried and without a direct heir, her royal cousin James VI of Scotland succeeded her on the English throne. Whereas the Tudor monarchs understood their relationship to the English Parliament, the royal Stuarts did not, and both James I (r. 1603–1625) and his son Charles I (r. 1625–1649) angered and frustrated Parliament with repeated violations of law and custom. Charles I's religious policies so antagonized the Calvinist Presbyterians in Scotland and English Puritans that large numbers of the devout became hostile to the monarchy. By 1637 the Scot Presbyterians were in open rebellion and, after repeated clashes between king and Parliament over policy, the long-simmering English Civil War broke out in 1642.

Early in 1642 Charles fled to the north of England and, in August, unfurled the royal standard at Nottingham. His cause was chiefly supported by the county militia of the north and west, and by the "Cavalier" faction of the aristocracy. His army was initially led by the Earl of Lindsey, an experienced but elderly soldier. The dashing Prince Rupert (1619–1682), Charles I's nephew, came from Holland to command the mounted arm. Parliament held the traditional capital at London, but its army was at first a loosely organized force consisting of associations of county militia and such professional soldiers as could be rallied to Parliament's cause. The Earl of Essex, the first Parliamentary commander-in-chief, was barely competent, but Parliament had the support of the navy and the Puritan "Roundheads" had the makings of excellent soldiers.

In the first phase of the war (1642–1643), both sides were short of arms and training, and tactics were rudimentary. Rupert's cavalry charges were successful against inexperienced Parliamentary troops where they might have failed against better disciplined and trained soldiers on the continent. Though Essex's 13,000 troops held Lindsey's 11,000 Royalists to a draw at the Battle of Edgehill in October 1642, Charles's army was able to seize Oxford as his capital and principal base for the rest of the war. In 1643 Charles's army bested Essex's army at the Battle of Newbury, and Rupert's forces captured Bristol, then the second-largest city in the kingdom. But the Royalists failed to exploit their advantage by undertaking an advance on London, and the tide turned decisively after Parliament's pact with the Scots in 1643.

In January 1644, an army of Scots under the Earl of Leven crossed the Tweed, cut off the royal garrison at Newcastle and laid siege to York. Rupert's 18,000 troops raised the siege in late June, but the Scots combined forces with Parliamentary troops and a total of 25,000 men faced Rupert's army on July 2 at the Battle of Marston Moor. In the biggest battle of the war, the Royalists were routed and some 4,000 of them killed in the fighting. The victory of the Parliamentarians and Scots was due in part to the excellent handling of the Parliamentary cavalry by Oliver Cromwell (1599–1658), only a few years removed from being a gentleman-farmer without military experience. After Marston Moor, the Royalist garrisons at York and Newcastle surrendered, and early in 1645 Charles and Parliament agreed to a truce in order to seek a negotiated end to the war.

Though negotiations with the king soon broke down, the lull permitted Parliament time in which to reorganize its forces in a "New Model Army," supported by regular taxation. The "New Model" was a semi-permanent force composed of 14,000 infantry, 6,600 cavalry, a thousand dragoons, and a few hundred artillerymen. Its chief officers were all proven campaigners, including Sir Thomas Fairfax, its commander in chief, Phillip Skippon, its Commanding General of Foot, and Cromwell, its Commanding General of Horse. (Among Cromwell's cavalry regiments were his formidable Puritan "Ironsides.") After hostilities resumed, the New Model Army struck a decisive blow against Charles's forces in June 1645 at the Battle of Naseby, another action in which Cromwell's generalship played a decisive role, and though the war dragged on, Naseby had really settled its outcome. Charles surrendered himself to the Scottish army in May 1646, and, in January 1647, the Scots remanded him to the custody of Parliament.

A long quarrel over Charles's fate and religious issues divided the English army, the Scots, and Parliament. When Parliament tried to dismiss the New Model Army in March 1647, its soldiers looked to Cromwell as their champion. Parliamentary negotiations with Charles were finally abandoned in January 1648, but the Scots rallied to his support. Another, if brief, war broke out when a Scottish army invaded England and Cromwell's forces trounced it at the Battle of Preston in August. In the following December, Cromwell's troops drove out all members from Parliament who favored royal restoration, then intimidated the Rump Parliament into indicting Charles on charges of treason. After he was found guilty, Charles was beheaded before his palace at Whitehall in January 1649.

## C. *The Commonwealth and the Restoration*

The regicide of 1649 left England officially the Commonwealth (a republic), but one that by degrees drifted into a full-fledged military-religious dictatorship. In 1653 Cromwell reduced the Rump Parliament to an even more compliant Barebones Parliament, and that December the army council made Cromwell the lord protector of the Commonwealth for life. In 1655 Cromwell abolished Parliament, divided England into military districts, and placed a major-general over each district to serve as its governor. He also expanded the standing army to 80,000 men. Though Cromwell's dictatorship could take credit for a revival of the English fleet, its gloomy internal policies and its bloody repression of revolts in Ireland and Scotland had secured it few friends by the time Cromwell died of natural causes in 1658.

Richard Cromwell succeeded his father as lord protector, but he resigned his post in less than a year. After a period of disorder, General George Monk seized control of the army council in February 1660, restored the Rump Parliament and supported its decision to pay off the army except for 5,000 troops. He also supported Parliament's decision to restore the monarchy on Parliament's terms and to invite Charles I's heir to return from exile on the continent. At the outset of the Restoration, Charles II (r.

1661–1685) appointed Monk captain-general of his army, bowed to the principle of Parliamentary supremacy, and seemed to respect the now deeply founded English suspicion of strong kings and standing armies.

## V. The Age of Louis XIV and Peter the Great

### A. Louis XIV, Vauban, and Marlborough

Louis XIV (r. 1661–1715), the greatest of the French Bourbon monarchs, so dominated events in western Europe in his time that a whole age has been called after him. His dominance was due in part to his possession of the most powerful European army of the age, which reached a peak strength in 1709 of 400,000 men, the largest European army before the French Revolution. Much of the credit for creating Louis's powerful army belongs to a succession of efficient ministers of war, especially the Marquis de Louvois, Louis's minister from 1668 to 1691. Among the reforms in Louis's army were the advent of inspectors-general responsible for auditing the army's accounts and eliminating waste and internal corruption; tables of organization that assigned specific duties to each officer from lieutenant to marshal; general improvements in training and discipline; and a logistical system that provided tents, bakeries, and an improved system of requisition for food and fodder.

The fortress depot was a major military factor in the patterns of war of an age in which most spare arms, ball, and powder could not be provided from current production and had to be systematically accumulated in the magazines of fortresses in peacetime. Sebastien le Prestre de Vauban (1633–1707), perhaps the greatest military engineer of his day, pioneered improved techniques for laying sieges, his system of parallels allowing for the systematic approach to the ramparts and bastions of an enemy fortress until enough artillery firepower could be assembled in protected positions to produce a breach. Perhaps even more important, in 1678 he drew up a scheme for the building of fortresses along France's frontiers that would serve as both barriers against foreign invasion and depots for offensive operations in neighboring countries. In their defensive role, they were to be large enough to force the enemy to divide his forces among a number of sieges, thereby allowing French forces of the interior to launch counter-offensives when the enemy was most vulnerable. Though Vauban died in 1707, his fortresses and strategic vision helped save northern France from invasion toward the end of the War of the Spanish Succession (1701–1714).

Infantry tactics changed over the course of Louis's reign as the flintlock musket gradually replaced the matchlock. The more efficient ignition system of the flintlock increased the firepower of musketry. At the same time, infantry gradually abandoned the pike in favor of variations of the bayonet—plug, ring, and, finally, socket—that made the flintlock musket an

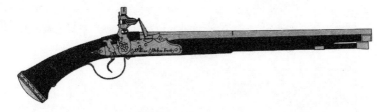

Flintlock Pistol, c. 1650.
William Reid, *Weapons Through the Ages* (New York: Crescent
Books, 1986 ed.), p. 126.

efficient combination fire-shock weapon. French infantry went over entirely
to the socket bayonet in 1703, a type with a sleeve that slid over the muzzle
and locked in place and which had an offset blade that permitted the
bayonet to remain fixed while the soldier loaded and fired. Other armies
followed suit, and, after the Battle of Malplaquet in 1709, the pike was
discarded by European armies. The combination of the flintlock musket
and bayonet led infantry to assume shallower formations in order that as
many men as possible at a time could fire, and the trend to linear deployment in the early eighteenth century caused infantry battalions to be formed
for battle in formations no deeper than three or four ranks. When threatened by hostile cavalry, they quickly formed into battalion "squares" for
all-round defense, each square typically six ranks to a side, the first three
ranks kneeling in order to form a hedge of bayonets to intimidate the
enemy's horses, and, in their rear, the other ranks standing and firing over
them.

### B. The Wars of Louis XIV

Louis XIV was responsible for four major wars during his reign, the first
two—the War of Devolution (1667–1678) and the Dutch War (1672–1678)—
aimed primarily at French expansion toward the Rhine and into the Low
Countries, and though these wars were not entirely successful in achieving
Louis's goals, the French armies were well-led in the persons of Marshal
Turenne and Prince Condé. But Turenne was killed in action in 1675, Condé
retired soon after, and, Vauban and possibly Marshal Villars aside, Louis
XIV was not served as well in the War of the League of Augsburg (1688–
1697) and in the War of the Spanish Succession (1701–1714).

Many of Louis's difficulties stemmed from the indefatigable efforts of
William of Orange, stadholder of the United Netherlands, who bent his
energies to form European alliances against French expansion. His marriage
to a daughter of the royal house of Stuart and the outcome of the Glorious
Revolution of 1688 in England allowed him to succeed James II (r. 1685–
1689) as William III. William and Mary presided over a dual Anglo-Dutch
monarchy that helped block Louis's ambitions in the War of the League of

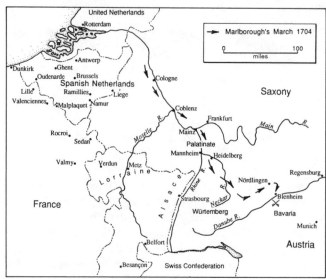

War of the Spanish Succession

Augsburg, and, even after Mary died in 1693 and William III died in 1702, Queen Anne (r. 1702–1714), William's sister-in-law, maintained England's alliance with the Dutch and opposition to Louis's ambitions in the War of the Spanish Succession.

The War of the Spanish Succession, the last and most important of Louis's wars, was brought about after Charles II, the last of the Spanish Habsburgs, died in 1700 without issue, and his will designated Philip of Anjou, Louis XIV's second grandson, as his heir. Accordingly, Philip V became the first of the Spanish Bourbon dynasty. The rest of Europe was willing to accept Philip V's accession until Louis XIV's actions made it fear the old danger of "universal monarchy," a fear once focused on the Habsburgs and now focused on the Bourbons. Louis alarmed Europe by granting Philip V and his descendants rights of succession to the French crown and by sending his troops to occupy the Spanish Netherlands and Spanish territories in Italy. He further antagonized William III by recognizing James the Pretender (the son of the dead James II, in exile) as the rightful monarch of England. In reaction, Leopold I of the Austrian Habsburg empire claimed the Spanish throne for his son, the Archduke Charles, declaring war on both France and Spain in 1701. England and Holland entered the fray in 1702. Eventually, the Grand Alliance against France and Spain consisted of England, Holland, Austria, Prussia, Portugal, Denmark, and, in the north of Italy, Savoy.

Upon England's intervention, John Churchill (1650–1722), Duke of Marlborough, was appointed captain-general of the confederated Anglo-Dutch army. A soldier who had seen service on the continent as far back as the Dutch War and who had survived the shifts of political fortune that had first elevated James II and then William II to the throne of England, Marl-borough was an astute politician as well as an able commander. Still, at the outset of his command, he was hampered by Dutch insistence that the safety of the Netherlands came before his cooperation with the Austrian Habsburgs, and this attitude helped to create a crisis for the allies when in the spring of 1704 a Franco-Bavarian army of 60,000 troops, commanded by Marshal Tallard, drove down the Danube in order to crush the Austrian forces under Prince Eugene of Savoy.

Marlborough saved the situation in 1704 by surprising his Dutch allies almost as much as his enemies. After making careful logistical preparations, he launched his army on a 250-mile march up the Rhine to Bavaria in order to link up with Eugene's forces in southern Germany. This feat accom-plished, the combined allied forces numbered 55,000 men, almost as many as were serving under Tallard. Marlborough then achieved his great victory at the Battle of Blenheim (Blindheim) in August by employing tactics that he so often used in the future. He launched attacks against one side of the enemy's line in order to draw his attention and reserves to that quarter, then made his main effort where he believed the enemy was weakest and most vulnerable. He was careful to see that his cavalry and infantry fought in mutual support, a practice that at Blenheim allowed them not only to parry a powerful French cavalry attack late in the day but also to mount a counterstroke that broke the center of the enemy's line and decided the outcome. At the battle's end, 34,000 of the enemy had been killed or cap-tured, and Tallard himself was a prisoner. Marlborough's casualties amounted to 12,000 men.

The outcome at Blenheim was followed by a French retreat, an Austrian occupation of Bavaria, and the return of Marlborough and his army to the defense of the Netherlands. Eugene went to northern Italy where allied forces under his command defeated the French at the Battle of Turin in 1706. Once back in Low Countries, Marlborough's army defeated Mar-shal Villeroi's offensive at Ramillies in 1707, and in 1708 Eugene joined Marlborough just in time to share in his victory over Marshal Vendôme's army at the battle of Oudenarde. But the greatest and bloodiest battle of the age occurred at Malplaquet in 1709 when 110,000 French troops under Marshal Villars engaged Marlborough's 90,000 troops in an effort to raise the siege of Mons. Though Marlborough defeated the French effort, the battle cost him a third of his army.

Having finally wrested the initiative from the French in the north, the allied army under Marlborough and Eugene sought to invade northern France in 1710–1711. The French army sheltered in a line of defenses dubbed the "Ne Plus Ultra" (none better) and eventually frustrated all allied efforts to get at Paris. Stretching for ninety miles between the river Canche on the channel coast and the city of Namur on the Sambre and constructed by many thousands of soldiers and peasants, the line consisted of defended rivers, morasses, redoubts and trenches, the whole anchored at intervals by the fortresses built earlier by Vauban and other French engineers. Though the allied army severely tested these defenses, the French capital remained secure until Marlborough's recall in December 1711. He never commanded in the field again. Prince Eugene succeeded him in command of the allied forces in the north, but in 1712 Marshal Villars' offensive caught the allied army divided, defeated part of it at the battle of Denain, and subsequently recovered most of the fortresses lost earlier to the allies. These events corresponded remarkably to Vauban's strategic vision dating back to 1678.

The War of the Spanish Succession was finally ended by a series of diplomatic compromises in 1713–1714 under the treaties of Utrecht, Rastatt, and Baden. Philip V kept his Spanish throne but agreed that the thrones of Spain and France were never to be united. Archduke Charles, who had become Emperor Charles VI on the death of his father in 1711, was compensated with most of Spain's empire in Europe, including the Spanish Netherlands (thereafter the Austrian Netherlands), Naples, Milan, and Sardinia. Savoy, after trading Sicily for Sardinia after the war, became the Kingdom of Sardinia-Piedmont. England probably gained the most from the war, having acquired an expanded overseas empire and a new degree of internal stability in the British isles. In Europe, England kept Gibraltar and Minorca, captured respectively in 1704 and 1708 and valuable in the future as naval bases.

### C. Russia and Peter the Great

Until the middle of the sixteenth century, the Russian army was essentially a feudal levy raised by the boyars (i.e., an aristocracy that ranked just below the princes) and the service nobility which held lands from the Tsar in return for performing military and administrative functions. In 1550 Ivan IV (the Terrible) made the first significant change in Russian military institutions by founding a corps called the *Streltsy* (musketeers), and, over its career, the corps numbered between 34,000 and 50,000 men. But the Streltsy meddled in dynastic matters and proved of little value in Russia's Time of Troubles (1598–1613) when the country was wracked by peasant insurrections and Polish and Swedish invasions. During the reign of Tsar Michael (1613–1645), the first of the Romanov dynasty, the traditional Russian forces were reinforced with regiments of foreign mercenaries, but none were kept up to strength or at a high level of discipline and training. Down to the reign of Peter I (1687–1725), Russia was not a very effective military power.

In 1697 Peter set out on his Great Embassy to the West in order to acquire the technical knowledge and foreign experts necessary to make Russia a modern power. Besides acquiring a personal knowledge of Western technology (for a time Peter worked with his own hands in a Dutch shipyard), he brought back to Russia a number of artisans and soldiers to help remodel

The Great Northern War, 1700 - 1721

Russia's industry and armed forces. In 1698 he seized on a mutiny of the Streltsy as an excuse to abolish the corps, and by 1700 his modest army of 32,000 troops was as "Westernized" as he could make it. The rank and file were mostly peasants who had escaped serfdom by volunteering for military service, and the officers were a mixture of Russians and foreigners, but the army was well-disciplined and equipped for the most part with up-to-date muskets and cannon, most of them produced by the new Russian factories. This force was to be the cornerstone of a much larger Russian army that was to prove both tough and effective.

The timing of Peter's reforms was propitious, for he was about to embark on a drive to the Gulf of Finland and the eastern Baltic Sea that was likely to involve Russia in war with the Swedish empire. Peter's dream was to build a new Russian capital at the head of the gulf as his "window on the West" and to create a battle fleet to command the Gulf and gain access to the Baltic. What became known as the Great Northern War was, however, not only of Peter's making. It was also generated by the ambitions of Augustus II, King of Poland and Elector of Saxony, and King Frederick IV of Denmark, both of whom were ready to league themselves with Peter in an effort to partition the Swedish empire. The three monarchs labored under the common delusion that Charles XII, the new nineteen-year-old king of Sweden, would be incapable of giving his country effective military leadership.

Actually, Charles XII was as remarkable as Peter himself and shared the martial instincts of his great uncle Gustavus Adolphus. He was also served by a formidable Swedish army and navy. Accordingly, in the years between 1700 and 1708, he defeated his Danish, Saxon, and Polish enemies and only failed to prevent Peter's army from occupying Livonia (Latvia), Ingria, and Estonia, or the Tsar founding a new capital at St. Petersburg (now Leningrad) at the mouth of the Neva. In January 1708, Charles XII led 45,000 veteran Swedish troops into Russia. Hindered first by winter conditions and then spring rains, Charles slowly made his way in the direction of Moscow. Unsure that his army was up to coping with the Swedes, Peter traded space for time and offered no major opposition before the Swedes crossed the Beresina river and captured Moghilev. At this critical juncture Charles accepted a proposal from Ivan Mezeppa, hetman of the Ukrainian Cossacks, that the Swedes postpone their attempt to capture Moscow, unite with 30,000 Cossacks in the Ukraine, and then resume the drive on Moscow in 1709.

Charles's diversion to the Ukraine proved to be a Swedish mistake and Peter's salvation. Mazeppa joined Charles with 8,000 men, not the 30,000 men he had promised, and the winter in the Ukraine proved to be unusually severe. By the spring of 1709 Charles's army had dwindled to 20,000 men, and most of these were preoccupied in a siege of Poltava. In June Peter led 40,000 troops close to the Swedish siege lines and placed them in a fortified camp. When Charles sought to deal with this threat by launching an assault on the Russian works with 7,000 men, half of them were killed or wounded by the Russian defenders. Peter then committed his force in a counterattack that ended by routing the whole of Charles XII's army. Only Charles, Mazeppa, and fewer than 2,000 of their troops managed to escape to the safety of Turkish Moldavia.

The destruction of Charles XII's army at the Battle of Poltava and Charles's temporary exile in the Ottoman Empire (he did not return to Sweden until 1715), turned the tide in the Great Northern War. Peter was enabled to launch operations in the north to recover Karelia, Livonia, Estonia, and Ingria, and to place Augustus II back on the throne of Poland by the end of 1709. Denmark and Prussia were emboldened to enter the alliance against Sweden. By the time Charles XII was back in Sweden, the Russians had occupied Finland, and a Russian fleet had insured Peter's control of the Gulf of Finland. Charles endeavored to regain the initiative by launching operations against the Danes, but a fatal bullet at the siege of Frederiksten in December 1718 cut short his career.

After the death of Charles XII, the Great Northern War gradually wound down. Queen Ulrika Eleonora, Charles's sister, made peace with Denmark and Prussia under the Treaty of Stockholm (1720), granting Schleswig to Denmark and the port of Stettin and part of Pomerania to Prussia. But under the Treaty of Nystadt (1721), Peter the Great emerged as the greatest winner in the Great Northern War. By the treaty's terms, Russia gained Livonia, Estonia, Ingria, part of Kerelia, and certain islands in the Baltic in exchange for Finland (except Vyborg) and a war indemnity. Perhaps equally important, by 1721, four years before Peter's death, Russia was recognized as the most powerful military state in eastern Europe.

### VI. The Patterns of Land Warfare, 1494–1721

Perhaps the most important pattern of war between the beginning of the Wars for Italy and the close of the Great Northern War, two and a quarter centuries later, was the evolution of the standing (or permanent) royal, dynastic army as the chief military instrument in Europe. As a military form in Europe, it eclipsed all others in effectiveness prior to the French Revolution of 1789. Second, the increasing use of gunpowder weapons gradually reduced all other weapons to a supporting role, and this trend most favored infantry which, by early in the eighteenth century, possessed an efficient fire-shock weapon in the flintlock musket and socket-bayonet combination. Third, after gunpowder artillery demolished the value of medieval fortifications in the fifteenth and early sixteenth centuries, engineers took their revenge on the gunners by designing fortresses, as represented in the *trace italienne,* especially resistant to the projectiles of smoothbore guns. Fortress design probably reached the peak of its effectiveness in the Age of Louis XIV and Vauban, by which time fortresses served not only as bulwarks of defense but, increasingly, as the chief supply depots for armies in the field.

Accordingly, the methods of fortification and siege became highly stylized, and most battles in the field pivoted on the siege and relief of fortresses. In the field, artillery still lacked much tactical mobility throughout this period, and the full development of even the muzzle-loading, smoothbore gun awaited the latter half of the eighteenth century. But especially from the middle of the seventeenth century on, the period saw important improvements in the internal administration and supply of armies, a growth in their size, and sometimes the skillful use of combined arms as, for example, in the generalship of Marlborough. As in previous periods of history, the great commanders of the period recognized the peculiar patterns of warfare of their time and adjusted to them better than their rivals.

# FIVE

# War under Sail
# and European Overseas
# Expansion to 1725

## I. The Early Sailing Navies and the Armada Campaign of 1588

### A. The Gunned Sailing Ship

Though the sailing ship had played a role in European naval warfare in the Middle Ages, the cog and similar European sailing vessels were too clumsy and without sufficient offensive power to replace the galley in pride of place as the most efficient tactical warship in the West. Even after the adoption of gunpowder weapons aboard vessels in the late Middle Ages, naval guns remained relatively small. The dominant warship in the Mediterranean Sea through most of the sixteenth century continued to be the galley, supplemented by the galleas, a hybrid oar-and-sail vessel with a gun deck above the rowers containing up to fifty small guns designed to kill men rather than to "kill" ships. Like the galley, the galleas was designed for the traditional tactics of "in-fighting" (ramming, grappling, and boarding). The last great action involving their types was the Battle of Lepanto (1571), off the Greek coast, in which a Spanish-Venetian-Papal fleet triumphed over a similar Turkish fleet.

Outside the Mediterranean, gunned sailing ships were quicker to establish dominance at sea in Europe, in part because they were larger than their medieval predecessors, equipped with multiple masts and sails, and capable of carrying more cargo, food, drink, and arms over longer distances. The carrack and the caravel, two of the more popular types in the sixteenth century, were essentially armed transports, but the galleon was more purely a sailing warship. Characterized by three or four masts, partly square-rigged, the galleon's chief armament in the first half of the sixteenth century consisted of numerous but small guns located in "castles" in its bow and stern, and a small number of "great guns" at its "waist" in so-called broadside batteries. An example of this sort of galleon was the English *Mary Rose* (1513), named after Henry VIII's sister and boasting five great guns on her main deck.

During Henry VIII's reign (1503–1547), the number of great guns per galleon in the English navy was increased, but galleons in the English and other navies remained more suited for "in-fighting" than "off-fighting" during the first half of the sixteenth century. Only in the latter half of the sixteenth century did the galleons of the various European navies begin to differ among themselves greatly. The transition to a main reliance on relatively large guns and the tactics of off-fighting occurred quicker in the English and Dutch navies than in the Spanish, but the process was a relatively slow one. Delay was imposed in part by the fact that a great gun weighed as much as 3,000 pounds, several times the weight of the smaller gun found in the ship's castles and thus represented an inordinate amount of metal in an age when the best guns were made of expensive bronze. Large iron guns were cheaper, but iron guns were more prone to develop invisible cracks that might cause them to blow up when fired. Another problem was that the main deck at the "waist" of the galleon was too encumbered with stores and gear for enough space to be found for many great guns. The shift to a primary reliance on great guns in broadside batteries and to the tactics of off-fighting required improvements in both metallurgy and in the design of ships.

In the English navy these improvements began to take place in the reign of Elizabeth I (1558–1603) as the quality of large iron guns improved (though iron guns were never as safe as bronze), and more space for large pieces in broadside was achieved by designing a galleon of deeper draft. The English built an orlop deck below the main deck at the water line to hold stores and gear, and increased the length of the main deck by reducing the castles for the smaller guns at either end. The first English galleon of the new design, appropriately named *Foresight*, displaced three hundred tons and was launched in 1570. She was followed by similar galleons, including *Revenge* (450 tons), the favorite ship of Sir Francis Drake, vice admiral of the English fleet. The English also rebuilt many of their older galleons along the lines of the newer ships, and by 1588 the warships in Elizabeth I's navy numbered thirty-four.

On the eve of the campaign of the Spanish Armada, an English galleon might carry as many great guns as a Spanish galleon of twice its displacement and was easier to bring about into the bargain. Maneuverability was especially important in an age of tactics when it was customary to discharge the guns on one side and then on the other, reloading while coming about. "We find by experience," Sir Walter Raleigh declared, " . . . [that] a ship of 600 tons will carry as good ordnance as a ship of 1,200 tons; . . . [for] though the greater [ship] have double her number of guns, the lesser will turn her broadsides twice before the greater can wind once, and so no advance [is achieved] in that overplus of ordnance [on the larger ship]." [Quoted in G. J. Marcus, *A Naval History of England: The Formative Centuries* (Boston and Toronto: Little, Brown and Company, 1961), p. 83.]

Though the Spanish Armada of 1588 was composed of 130 vessels, and

the English fleet 197, most of the ships on both sides were converted trans-
port, supply, and liaison craft. The true fighting power in each fleet lay in
the best forty-five vessels on each side, both galleons and armed transports,
and here the English advantage is clear. The English ships averaged a
displacement of four hundred tons and mounted an average of thirty-six
guns, and their combined broadsides came to 7,000 pounds of shot. The
best forty-five Spanish ships, though they averaged almost eight hundred
tons, mounted an average of thirty guns, and had combined broadsides
of 4,500 pounds of shot. The English guns on average outranged the Spanish, and, though the Armada as a whole carried 24,000 men compared to
16,000 in the English fleet, more than half the men aboard the Spanish
ships were soldiers, useless in a sea fight unless their ships could get close
enough to the English ships for them to grapple and board, the very tactics
that the English ships were designed to avoid.

### B. The Armada Campaign of 1588

Philip II's "Invincible Armada" required four years to assemble at Lisbon
(seized by the Spanish during their occupation of Portugal in 1580), and
it left that port to take part in the invasion of England in May 1588. Under
the command of the Duke of Medina-Sidonia, a professional soldier rather
than a sailor, it rewatered at Corunna and arrived at the Channel at the
end of July. It formed a crescent-shaped formation, the most powerful ships
on the outer edges, and set a course for Calais, Medina-Sidonia planning
to anchor his fleet there until joined by the rest of the invasion force, a
flotilla of small craft bearing troops, forming under the Duke of Parma at
Nieuport and Dunkirk. Once Medina-Sidonia and Parma united their
forces, the Spanish would set forth for a landing in the estuary of the
Thames.

The Armada, 1588.
Jan de Hartog, *The Sailing Ship* (New York: Odyssey Press, 1964),
pp. 16–17.

When the Armada appeared in the Channel, the English fleet, commanded by Lord Howard of Effingham and seconded by Drake, was mostly concentrated at the port of Plymouth. Adverse winds hindered the English fleet's attempts to get to sea and, when it finally entered the Channel, it was behind the Armada and had to press on sail in order to catch up. Then a slow-moving fight ensued that lasted four days (on one of which the two fleets lay becalmed), the English ships harrying the fringes of the slow-moving Spanish formation but staying at such a distance that their fire, as well as the Spanish, was mostly ineffective. Both sides used up prodigious quantities of ammunition, the Spanish alone consuming 100,000 rounds.

The two fleets arrived off Calais relatively unscathed, the Spanish fleet anchoring in the roads and the English fleet anchoring to seaward out of range, and the fatal hitch in Spanish plans came when shallow-drafted Dutch craft blocked the channels leading out of Dunkirk and Nieuport, preventing Parma's forces from getting to sea. While Parma was thus stymied, on the night of August 6–7 the English fleet launched eight fireships (vessels loaded with combustibles, lighted, and set adrift) against the anchored Armada. The Spanish ships managed to dodge the fireships by slipping their anchor cables, but the attack forced Medina-Sidonia to take his force to sea again. Medina-Sidonia steered in the direction of Nieuport and Dunkirk, but in fighting off Calais and Gravelines on August 7–8, the English closed to effective gun range, inflicting heavy damage on many Spanish ships. At the end of the battle only seven Spanish ships had been sunk or taken since the Armada entered the Channel on July 31, but the Armada had been severely handled and had drifted into the North Sea.

Once in the North Sea, Medina-Sidonia made up his mind to abandon the attempt to invade England in 1588 and to return his fleet to Spain. The most direct route was by the Channel, but he did not relish another fight with the English by attempting to return the way he had come. The English fleet continued to shadow the Armada as it withdrew ever deeper into the North Sea, and, even though the English fleet turned away on August 12 and disappeared, Medina-Sidonia assumed that it would remain between the Armada and its natural line of retreat. Actually, outbreaks of scurvy and typhus—and lack of food, water, and ammunition—had forced most of the English ships to head for port. Had the Armada reversed course after August 12 and headed for the Channel, it might have stood a chance of reaching Spain without a fight.

The English fleet's whereabouts being unknown, Medina-Sidonia decided to return to Spain by sailing around the British isles, taking the Atlantic route home. The decision doomed his fleet. Off the coasts of Scotland and Ireland his fleet was beset by fierce storms for days on end, causing many of the Spanish ships to founder or to be driven ashore to their destruction, and even those ships that made it to Spanish ports were often half-filled with dead and dying men. Medina-Sidonia's ship survived to reach a Spanish port on September 23, and the duke lived long enough to report his failure to Philip II, but he too died not long afterwards. All told, the Armada lost sixty-three of its ships (48%) and about 16,000 of its men (66%), losses far higher than the English. Perhaps the most striking aspects of the whole enterprise were that acts of nature had taken more lives and ships than fighting and that neither the Armada nor the English fleet proved up to the demands of a long campaign.

## II. Navies of the Seventeenth and Eighteenth Centuries

### A. The Evolution of Warship Design

In 1610 England commenced a revolution in warship architecture by launching *Prince Royal,* the first sailing warship with two gun-decks below the main deck running the entire length of the vessel. This prototype of the ship-of-the-line-of-battle (or ship of the line, for short) carried in excess of sixty large guns in broadside batteries. In 1637 England launched the even more powerful *Sovereign of the Seas,* a ship with three gun decks below the main deck and carrying more than eighty large guns. Other countries soon followed England's lead in building ships of the line with two and three gun decks, and those types became the battleships of the age. Vessels "below-the-line," or those with fewer than sixty guns, were considered too lightly armed to serve against enemy battleships and were used for auxiliary duties such as escorting convoys of merchantships, preying on enemy commerce at sea, and supporting amphibious assaults. The main types below-the-line in the eighteenth century were the frigate and the sloop-of-war, a typical frigate having thirty-two guns and one gun deck. A sloop-of-war carried about twenty guns on her main deck.

Though a few larger ships of the line were built, the practical upper limit was about 3,500 tons displacement, three gun decks, and about 120 guns. A "first rate" in the British navy of the eighteenth century carried in excess of a hundred guns, had a length of almost two hundred feet, a maximum beam of fifty feet, and a height from keel to main deck of about forty feet (equivalent to that of a four-story building without its roof). As many as eight hundred to a thousand men might be required to operate such a ship efficiently, most of the manpower needed to man the guns. A more typical ship of the line in the eighteenth century was the seventy-four gunner, displacing about 2,000 tons, with two gun decks and manned by about six hundred men. There were, of course, many variations, but no ship of the line carried fewer than sixty guns.

Whereas the largest gun found in broadside in English ships in 1588 was the eighteen pounder (5.3-inch bore), the broadside batteries of the seventeenth and eighteenth centuries included eighteen pounders, twenty-four pounders (5.84-inch bore), and thirty-two pounders (6.4-inch bore). Smaller guns (twelve-pounders and nine-pounders) might be mounted on

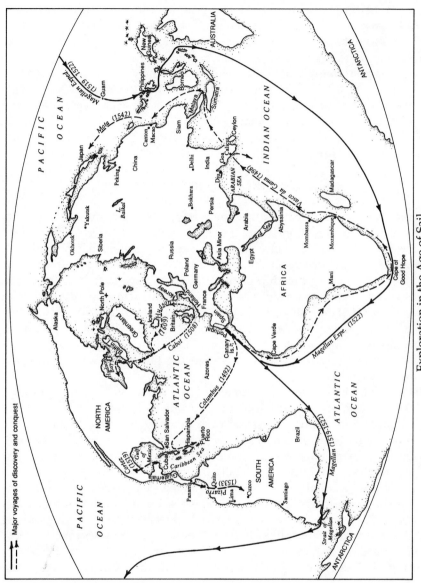

Exploration in the Age of Sail

the quarter deck, the main deck, and on the deck of the forecastle to supplement the fire of the main batteries. With its truck, the thirty-two pounder, the largest gun carried in broadside, weighed three tons and required a crew of nine to operate efficiently. The other large guns required smaller crews, but none required fewer than five men. The theoretical range of a thirty-two pounder was about three miles, but the gun's lack of rifling, the pitch and roll of the ship, and the crude aiming devices available made accurate fire almost impossible at ranges over a thousand yards. In order for as many guns as possible to take part, battles were usually fought within 500 yards of the enemy and individual vessels sometimes fought it out yardarm to yardarm.

## B. Fleet Tactics under Sail

In theory, a fleet of battleships could engage the enemy in a variety of ways in the Age of Sail, including the line-abreast formation as in the days of the galley, especially with the helter-skelter attitude that prevailed in the English and Dutch navies until the middle of the seventeenth century. But the square rig of the ship of the line, its relative lack of firepower in its bows compared to its sides, and the growing size of battleships with less maneuverability all combined to make the old tactics less feasible, especially coming about between broadsides. With the newer goliaths, it was more practicable to step up the rate of fire of the guns already engaged, and this practice, in turn, recommended the line-ahead as the most appropriate formation.

The shift to the line-ahead commenced in the English fleet in March 1653 when the admiralty issued fighting instructions for initial contact with the enemy; the ships were to provide each other with mutually supporting fire. The Dutch soon imitated the English example, and other navies followed suit. For greater ease of command, a fleet in line-ahead was commonly divided into divisions, usually three—the van, the center, and the rear—and the admiral and vice admiral commanded respectively either the van or the center divisions, and, of course, the rear admiral commanded the trailing division. The normal interval between battleships when sailing in line-ahead was about three hundred yards. A large fleet might stretch out for miles while moving at the stately pace of six knots an hour. Orders and reports at sea were communicated to and from the "flag ships" (the headquarters ships of the admirals), and to and from the captains of the individual ships, by signal flags in daylight hours and by hoisting lanterns at night. The naval telescope—adopted over the course of the seventeenth century—became a great aid in observing signals and the movements of the enemy.

In engagements between fleets in line-ahead, the weather gauge (upwind of the enemy) was considered the offensive position, and in the Anglo-Dutch Wars discussed below, both the English and Dutch fleets often sought to seize the weather gauge and initiate action. By the beginning of the eighteenth century, however, the English fleet (after 1707 the British fleet) had such a commanding lead in numbers of battleships that in most fleet actions its opponents conceded it the weather gauge and sought to fight in the lee from where they might more easily retreat if a reverse was suffered. In the eighteenth century, a school of admirals in the British navy called formalists insisted on maintaining "conterminous line" (line-ahead and parallel to the enemy line) under nearly all conditions, while another school called the meleeists held that divisions and individual ships should be free to depart from the line when they saw an opportunity to break up the enemy's formation. Forcing a melee could be accomplished by breaking (penetrating a gap in the enemy's line), massing (concentrating one's ships against a segment of the enemy line), or doubling (attempting to get ships on both sides of the enemy's line and putting it in a crossfire), but experience demonstrated that such "melee tactics" were also very risky. By the early eighteenth century, the more cautious formalists had the upper hand in the British navy and the effects of their rigidity is discussed in more detail in the next chapter.

### III. England's Rise to Naval Supremacy

#### A. The Anglo-Dutch Wars

The Spanish navy went into decline after Spain's sources of gold and silver in America were exhausted in the first half of the seventeenth century, but neither England nor France filled the resulting void at sea. Down to the English Civil War (1642–1648), the English navy was weakened by quarrels between the Stuart kings and Parliament over the fleet's financing, and the fleet's recovery did not get underway until the rule of Oliver Cromwell at mid-century. As for France, Henry IV laid the foundations of a permanent French navy during his reign (1589–1610), but French naval policy was so inconsistent and France was so involved in continental affairs that at the commencement of Louis XIV's personal rule in 1661 the fleet had declined to three ships of the line and twenty-seven lesser warships. Jean-Baptiste Colbert, Louis XIV's able minister of finance, launched a massive rebuilding of the French fleet, but the full fruits of his program were not fully realized until late in the century.

Perforce, the United Provinces of the Netherlands (hereafter referred to as Holland, the largest of the provinces and furnishing five-sixths of the Dutch fleet) succeeded Spain as the paramount European sea power, a position the Dutch did not fully surrender until the century was three-quarters over. Though a nation of only two million people by 1650, the Dutch possessed, besides a battle fleet, a merchant marine that nearly monopolized Europe's carrying trade and an overseas empire that included colonies in North America, posts on the coasts of Africa (including Cape Colony), and islands in the East Indies. But the most valuable Dutch resource was its near monopoly over the European carrying trade, an advantage that was threatened when Cromwell's regime adopted the Navigation Act of 1651. The Act allowed only English ships to carry English goods and denied entry to English ports to Dutch ships carrying the cargoes of third countries. To the Dutch this was an intolerable situation, and in May 1652 Holland declared a state of war with the English Commonwealth.

The focus of the First Anglo-Dutch War (1652–1654) was on the North Sea, the Straits of Dover, and the English Channel, all vital to the flow of trade between Holland and her customers. Despite a series of hard-fought naval battles between the fleet of the English Commonwealth and the Dutch fleet, the First Anglo-Dutch War was at a stand off until the summer of 1653. Then the English fleet of about a hundred ships under George Monk (one of Cromwell's Generals-at-Sea) engaged a Dutch fleet of similar size under Admiral Martin Tromp off the island of Texel near the Dutch coast, and, operating under the new fighting instructions discussed in a previous section, won the first true line-ahead action in history in twelve hours of bloody fighting. Tromp and 1,500 fellow Dutch sailors were killed, fourteen Dutch ships were lost, and the rest of the Dutch fleet was forced to seek safety in port. After an English blockade faced Holland with economic ruin, the Dutch ended the war in April 1654 by recognizing the terms of the Navigation Act, paying England a war indemnity, and making colonial concessions.

The Second Anglo-Dutch Naval War (1665–1667) followed the Stuart Restoration, Charles II's ascent to the throne, and Charles's official redes-

Sea Battle, c. 1650, Anglo-Dutch Wars.
Jan de Hartog, *The Sailing Ship* (New York: Odyssey Press, 1964),
pp. 20–21.

ignation of the English fleet as the Royal Navy. The causes of the war were Parliament's adoption of a revised Navigation Act that largely barred the Dutch from serving as carriers of the trade in the English colonies, combined with an undeclared war against the Dutch empire overseas in which, among other places, the English captured New Amsterdam in 1664 and renamed it New York in honor of the Duke of York, the Royal Navy's Lord High Admiral. When formal war broke out between England and Holland in January 1665, the focus of the conflict at sea was again on the North Sea, the Straits of Dover, and the Channel.

As in the first Anglo-Dutch conflict, the fate of Holland rested with the ability of the Dutch fleet to keep open its sea lanes, and the Dutch fought vigorously to do so. One of the biggest naval battles ever fought under sail occurred off the English coast at Lowestoft in June 1665 when Lord Opdam (or Obdam) and a Dutch fleet of 103 vessels engaged an English fleet of 109 ships of the line under James, Duke of York, in an action that lasted most of a day. Before its conclusion, Opdam's flagship blew up, and thirty-one other Dutch ships had been destroyed or taken. After the surviving Dutch fleet retreated to port, the English imposed a blockade on the Dutch coasts, and the second Anglo-Dutch War seemed certain to end like the first with a Dutch capitulation to English terms.

But matters went differently in the second Anglo-Dutch War. In January 1666 Louis XIV brought France into the conflict against England, and though France had only about twenty ships of the line, the threat of a hostile fleet-in-being at the channel forced the English navy to divide its forces. The Dutch were able once more to escort convoys bearing vital trade, and in a particularly fierce action in the Channel and the Straits of Dover, known as the Four Day's Battle, (June 1666) a Dutch fleet commanded by Admiral Michael de Ruyter defeated an English fleet commanded by Monk (by then the Duke of Albemarle) and drove it into the Thames. But Albemarle effected speedy repairs, and in July his fleet sortied forth to win a smashing victory over de Ruyter's forces in the St. James's Day Battle off the North Foreland. At the cost of a single English ship, Albemarle's fleet sank or captured twenty of de Ruyter's ships and forced the Dutch fleet to retreat into port.

Still, the Dutch stubbornly refused to give in, the war dragged on, and by 1667 Charles II was in such financial difficulty that, against Albemarle's advice, he ordered much of his fleet returned to the Thames and Medway, the crews paid off, and the ships left at their moorings. De Ruyter seized the opportunity in June to descend with his fleet on the immobilized English force and to destroy or capture several of Charles's helpless vessels. This English humiliation was followed a month later by a treaty whereby England modified the Navigation Act in favor of the Dutch, traded some colonial chips for others, but retained New York.

At the commencement of the Third Anglo-Dutch War in 1672, England and France were allies against the Dutch. A large Anglo-French fleet of 101 ships assembled in Southwolde Bay (Solebay), ninety miles north of the Thames, preparatory to cooperation with the French armies about to invade the United Provinces. Just as the allied fleet was leaving port, Admiral de Ruyter's seventy ships suddenly appeared and, in modern terminology, launched a preemptive strike. The Dutch fell with such a fury on the English contingent, commanded by the Duke of York and poorly supported by the French, that only by dint of hard fighting were the English able to hold the Dutch to a tactical standoff. The strategic outcome of that battle delayed Anglo-French domination of the sea for some time, but Holland was ultimately no match for the Anglo-French powers combined. By 1674 the Dutch had been forced to lay up so many ships in order to release men and guns to the hard-pressed Dutch army that the Anglo-French fleets were able to impose a blockade on the Dutch coasts. As Dutch trade vanished, hunger stalked the Netherlands.

Fortunately for the Dutch, the Anglo-French alliance against Holland collapsed when Parliament—outraged by its discovery that Charles II had been secretly on Louis XIV's payroll since the Treaty of Dover (1670)—forced the king to make peace with Holland. Under the treaty, the Dutch were required to return New York (recaptured in 1673) to English control, but otherwise they did not fare too badly. Moreover, the Dutch fleet revived enough to reopen Holland's sea lanes and to help make it possible to reach acceptable terms with France in 1678. Still, the Third Anglo-Dutch War had taken its toll of Dutch strength, and Holland never regained her former naval or commercial position in Europe.

### B. The Naval Wars with Louis XIV

As mentioned in the previous chapter, England and Holland, formerly bitter enemies, became allies when William and Mary succeeded to the throne of England following the "Glorious Revolution" of 1688. But hardly had the Anglo-Dutch monarchy been formed than it was challenged by the formidable power of Louis XIV. In the War of the English Succession (a part of the wider War of the League of Augsburg, 1688–1697), Louis XIV was bent on overthrowing William III, restoring Catholic James II to the English throne, and destroying the independence of the Protestant Dutch.

The naval phase of the War of the English Succession began in the French favor in March 1690 when a French naval squadron eluded the English and Dutch fleets and landed James II in Ireland in order that he might lead the Irish Catholics against William III's rule. William III, his army, and part of his fleet moved to Ireland in order to suppress the rebellion, and by the summer of 1690 the defense of England against a French invasion rested almost entirely with an Anglo-Dutch channel fleet of fifty-six ships of the line commanded by the Earl of Torrington. But seventy French ships of the line under Count de Tourville lay at Brest, and Tourville did not miss the opportunity. In July 1690, the same month in which William III's forces defeated those of James II at the Battle of the Boyne in Ireland, Tourville's fleet heavily defeated Torrington's fleet off Beachy Head in a battle in which Torrington lost sixteen ships. The weakened Anglo-Dutch fleet retreated to the Thames and, in its absence, the French fleet commanded the Channel. Had the French army been ready to take advantage of the situation by launching an invasion of England, the further history of Europe, and of the world, might have been very different.

But the French army was not prepared for a cross-channel invasion in 1690, Tourville's victory proved transitory, and by the spring of 1692, when Louis XIV had collected 30,000 troops for an invasion effort, the Channel was guarded by an Anglo-Dutch fleet of ninety-nine ships of the line under Admiral Edward Russell. By then much of the French fleet had been transferred to the Mediterranean, and Tourville was counting heavily on its return to Brest to give him the necessary numbers to insure success in the looming struggle. When adverse winds delayed the arrival of the reinforcements from the Mediterranean, Tourville's fleet put to sea with only forty-four ships of the line. Not surprisingly, and despite skillful tactics on Tourville's part, the French fleet was defeated in the Battle of Cape de la Hogue (or Barfleur) off the tip of the Normandy peninsula in May 1692. The French defeat, and its aftermath, cost Tourville fifteen ships of the line and Louis XIV any hope of ever commanding the Channel.

But the outcome at Cape de la Hogue had ramifications that went far beyond the War of the English Succession. After his naval reverses in 1692, Louis XIV gave little financial support to the French fleet and preoccupied himself with his continental wars. In contrast, the English fleet flourished. By the time England and Scotland were formally joined in the United Kingdom of Great Britain in 1707, the British navy had assumed a supremacy to any likely combination of enemies. During the War of the Spanish Succession, and with the Dutch fleet allied to the British, the British fleet was more than a match for the Franco-Spanish fleet combined. Most of the fighting took the form of Anglo-Dutch attacks on French and Spanish convoys moving surreptitiously at sea, actions between Anglo-Dutch warships and enemy raiders waging *guerre de course* (commerce raiding), and operations to seize or defend posts and colonies. Nor in any subsequent war during the Age of Sail, except to a degree during the War of the American Revolution, was Britain's command of the sea ever seriously threatened. Therefore, it has been said that before the battle of Cape de la Hogue England was *a* seapower, after the battle *the* seapower, a position she was to retain well beyond the end of the Age of Sail.

## IV. European Overseas Expansion and Conquest

### A. The Orient

Besides its greater range and firepower compared to earlier vessels, the early modern sailing ship benefitted from improved means of navigation.

European mariners had borrowed the magnetic compass from the Arabs in the Middle Ages, and by the fifteenth and sixteenth centuries they were employing the sea quadrant, astrolabe, and cross staff for determining a ship's latitude by calculating the height of celestial bodies (e.g., the North Star) above the horizon. They lacked a scientific means for calculating longitude until the eighteenth century and the advent of accurate naval chronometers, but, as the experiences of many voyages were incorporated into nautical charts and sailing instructions, gradually the global range of the sailing ship was exploited to make the Europeans masters of distant realms. For a long time the gunned sailing ship was their principal advantage over non-European rivals.

As early as the fifteenth century, the gunned sailing ship and the improved means of navigation emboldened the Portuguese mariners to seek a new passage to the Orient by sailing around Africa in order to avoid the Muslim-dominated eastern Mediterranean. The Portuguese proceeded by stages down the west African coast, an expedition under Bartholomew Diaz finally reaching the Cape of Good Hope and the Indian Ocean in 1488. Between 1497 and 1499 a Portuguese expedition under Vasco da Gama made the first European round trip between Portugal and India by way of

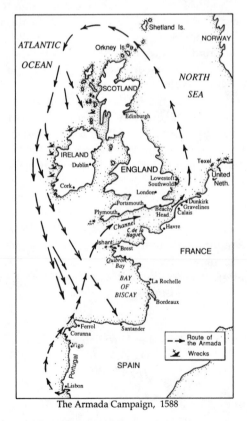

The Armada Campaign, 1588

the Cape. After da Gama's expedition returned to Portugual with a cargo of rich spices, fleets of armed Portuguese trading ships began using the route by the Cape to engage in commerce with India, activity that stimulated the Portuguese to establish way stations on both coasts of Africa. Portuguese naval superiority in Indian waters was established in 1509 when their guns defeated a fleet of Muslim galleys off Diu, and in 1510 the Portuguese established Goa as the capital for their coastal trading empire in India.

In 1511 a Portuguese expedition captured Malacca at the straits between Malaya and Sumatra at the eastern end of the Indian Ocean, and between 1512 and 1514 other Portuguese expeditions established themselves in the Moluccas (the fabled "Spice Islands") in the Pacific Ocean. Portuguese expeditions sailed from thence to the Chinese coast, where they extorted the colony of Macao and trading rights at Canton from the Ming dynasty. They also colonized the great island of Taiwan (called Formosa by the Portuguese), and soon established a trading mission in Japan. But the Spanish subsequently ousted the Portuguese from Taiwan and the East Indies, and, in turn, the Spanish were driven out of those places by the Dutch. A native rebellion in the seventeenth century drove the Dutch out of Taiwan, but they remained in the Dutch East Indies—modern Indonesia—down to the era of World War II.

That Japan managed to avoid European colonization in the sixteenth and seventeenth centuries was largely due to the ability of the Takagawa Shogunate to quell internal wars among the *daimyos* (the feudal lords) and the *samurai* (Japan's hereditary warrior class) and to present a united front to the West. The Shogun also took firm action to discourage Western trade and influence, and from about the mid-seventeenth century to 1853 only the Dutch, among the Western peoples, were permitted to have a trade mission in Japan. Japan had survived a long period of disorder after the collapse of the Yamato rule in the fourth century, and, though the emperor secreted at Kyoto was treated as divine, beginning in 1192 real power was exercised in his name by the Shogun ("Barbarian-subduing general in chief"). By this time the samurai had emerged as a privileged warrior class especially skilled in the use of a long-bladed, highly tempered sword made of steel. The samurai was bound by the code of *Bushido* (Way of the Warrior) that set forth the obligations of its members, which included fighting for one's lord until death and ritual suicide in case of failure. With the help of the samurai and timely typhoons, the Japanese repelled Chinese invaders in 1274 and 1281, and the tradition of the Kamikaze (Divine Wind) entered Japanese folklore. Though internal order in Japan had broken down by the time the Portuguese arrived in the sixteenth century, the Takagawa Shogunate restored the solidity of Japanese society to the point that isolation from the West was maintained until 1853. The Takagawa Shogunate itself was not ended until 1867.

Until well into the eighteenth century, the western European empires in the Orient were confined to islands and coastal areas, and the continental states of Asia, as long as they maintained their internal cohesion, lay beyond their control. Besides the fact that power based on gunned sailing ships could not as easily intimidate continental states as island countries, the Europeans in the Orient were numerically few; as late as 1750 there were about 20,000 Europeans in India and Southeast Asia when the populations of India and China were respectively about 100 million apiece. But when internal factors caused the Mogul Empire in India to disintegrate in the mid-eighteenth century, the Europeans exploited the divisions and struggled among themselves for dominance in the sub-continent. The British East India Company eventually became the paramount power there. In the mid-nineteenth century, India became a British crown colony, and the *raj* (British rule) over most of the sub-continent would not finally end until 1947.

Ming China arose after the collapse of Mongol rule, and, though the Ming emperors virtually abandoned the sea after 1430, they managed to make relatively small concessions to the western Europeans in respect to trade and colonization. Among other things, they demanded, and received, gold for anything the Westerners bought in China. The greater threat to the Ming came from the north where the Manchus, a confederation of tribes, seized control of Manchuria. In order to contain Manchu expansion, the Ming emperors relied heavily on the Great Wall, which they significantly extended in their reign and which largely served its purpose until civil war divided the Chinese. In 1644 the Manchus penetrated the defenses of the Great Wall, captured the Ming capital at Peking (Beijing), and eventually extended their control over the whole of China. The Ching dynasty, founded by the Manchus, lasted until 1911.

### B. The Conquest of Latin America

On September 6, 1492, a Spanish expedition of three ships under the command of the Italian Christopher Columbus left the Canary Islands and undertook to find a western route to the Orient across the Atlantic ocean. Grossly underestimating the size of the earth, Columbus believed that Asia was no more that 4,000 miles west of Europe. Likewise, he had no inkling that a continent separated the Atlantic from the Pacific ocean. After sailing west for nearly 3,000 miles, his expedition made landfall on October 12 in what he believed to be islands in the East Indies, whereupon, and incorrectly, he dubbed the natives "Indians." His discovery turned out to be islands in the Carribean Sea at the threshold of the New World of America. After Columbus's mistake was recognized, the Carribean region was dubbed the West Indies.

Spain and Portugal agreed in 1494 to a north-south line in the Atlantic west of which all newly-discovered territory would belong to Spain and that to the east would belong to Portugal. After the subsequent discovery of South America, the treaty placed Brazil in the Portuguese sphere. Elsewhere in the New World Spain was for a long time the predominant power, exploring and claiming Cuba, Santo Domingo, Puerto Rico, much of South America, Central America, Mexico, the southwest of the North American continent, the peninsula of Florida, and some points further north on the eastern seaboard of North America. After Ferdinand Magellan's expedition carried out the first circumnavigation of the globe between 1519 and 1522, sailing from east to west across the Pacific, Spain also took title to Guam and the Philippines, the latter to serve as a base of trade with China.

The importance of the gunned sailing ship to the European seizure of the West Indies and other island territories is too obvious to belabor, but this technical advantage does not explain the rapid Spanish conquest of the continental Aztec empire in Mexico (estimated population 27 million) or that of the empire of the Incas in Peru, Bolivia and part of Chile (estimated population 11 million). Nor does the European monopoly on land firearms fully explain the outcome. The number of Europeans in these expeditions were simply too few for the firearms of the day to have made that much impression. Hernando Cortez's conquest of Mexico between 1519 and 1521 was undertaken with just six hundred troops, and just 150 Europeans accompanied Francisco Pizarro in his conquest of the empire of the Incas about ten years later. Part of the answer is that the Europeans found the Indians divided among themselves and an easy prey to treachery. Many were available for recruitment for Spanish purposes. Beyond dispute is the demographic disaster brought upon the Indian population by the European arrival. Though slavery and social dislocation took their toll, the diseases that accompanied the Europeans and their black African slaves (and against which the Indians had no natural immunity) were chiefly responsible for a drop in the Latin American Indian population from an estimated 57 million in 1492 to six million people about a century later. By way of comparison, the six years of World War II caused the deaths of an estimated 55 million people over the whole globe.

## C. The Conquest of Eastern North America

The European conquest of the eastern seaboard of North America was both slower to take place and took a different form from that in Latin America. Except for outposts in Florida, including St. Augustine (1565), and a few forts on the coasts of the Carolinas further north, which were eventually abandoned, Spain took less interest in this region than other areas in the New World. Thus, the French were free to settle Maine (1604), Acadia or Nova Scotia (1605), and Quebec (1608) as "New France" or Canada, and, after an English failure to establish a permanent colony on the coast of North Carolina in the 1580s, a surviving colony was founded at Jamestown in Virginia (1607). The Dutch established a trading post on Manhattan island (1612) from which evolved the town of New Amsterdam and the colony of the New Netherlands that included territory in the future states of New York, New Jersey, and Delaware. In 1620, after it was blown off course by storms and missed its destination of Virginia, the *Mayflower* landed the Puritan Pilgrims at the future site of Plymouth in Massachusetts, the first of the colonies in New England. By 1650 the English had established additional colonies in Connecticut, Rhode Island, and Maryland, and in 1670 they founded Charlestowne (Charleston) in South Carolina. Georgia, the last of the original thirteen English colonies in North America, was founded in the eighteenth century.

The number of English colonies in North America proliferated in part because of migration and in part because of English seizure of other colonies. The New Netherlands, for instance, became English territory over the course of the seventeenth century, and Canada fell to the British during the eighteenth century. The tolerant English policy on immigration encouraged many nationalities to enter the English colonies and contributed to their variety as well as to their rapid growth. Most of the Europeans coming to the New World colonies of other countries were either adventurers bent on quick profit and a swift return to Europe or were barred or restricted by religious preference. The relatively easy rule and religious tolerance in the English colonies encouraged a variety of European immigrants to come to stay as small farmers, artisans, and tradesmen. Except in the southern colonies, they did not emulate the practice in the West Indies of establishing plantations worked by black slaves, nor, for the most part, did they attempt to enslave the North American Indian. By 1725 English North America was characteristically a land of small farms, villages, and towns in which labor was performed by free men and indentured European servants.

The sheer growth of population in the English colonies gave them an edge over both the competing European colonies and the native North American Indians. Though a fairly advanced Indian civilization had once existed beyond the Appalachian mountains, it had disappeared before the Europeans arrived in North America, and the Indians on the eastern seaboard were comparatively primitive. The Indian population of North America by the eighteenth century probably did not exceed half a million people when, in contrast, the population of the English colonies in North America was already 400,000 by 1725. It was more than six times greater at the outbreak of the American Revolution, fifty years later. The Indians were also inferior in weapons except when the Europeans supplied them with firearms and ammunition, and they proved incapable of uniting politically. Indeed, they were often found on opposing sides in the European wars for North America. In consequence, Indian resistance slowed, but never contained, European expansion in North America.

Finally, British command of the sea was of enormous importance to the survival of the English colonies against their competitors, especially from the late seventeenth century on. In time of war, British command of the sea allowed the movement of reinforcements and supplies from the home country to aid an embattled colony in a way not usually available to Britain's rivals in Europe. Yet, the English population in the colonies was large enough to raise militia for local defense and to negate the need for large regular garrisons in peacetime. The forests and the deposits of pitch and tar in certain of the English colonies proved valuable assets to a wooden navy, and the trade and commerce that developed between Britain and her colonies became a major source of her wealth and power.

# SIX

# The Patterns of
# Neoclassical War, 1725–1789

### I. Land Warfare in the Neoclassical Age

The patterns of early modern land warfare that had been evolving since the late fifteenth century reached their culmination in the middle decades of the eighteenth century in what might be termed the Neoclassical age. In this period, the art of war lay in the skillful use of old rules rather than in the invention of new ones in the pursuit of royal or dynastic goals, and the age was marked by relative stability in the conduct of war. This stability would begin to crumble with the onset of the American Revolution, beginning in 1775, but the era really ended after the outbreak of the French Revolution of 1789. Just as Europe took on new political contours after 1789, it also took on new military contours during the Wars of the French Revolution and Napoleon (1792–1815). Thus the Neoclassical age turned out to be the swan song of early modern warfare and the precursor to the age of national warfare.

### A. The Social-Political Character of the Neoclassical Army

Down to the eve of the French Revolution, the armies of continental Europe remained reflections of a hierarchical society in which royal power and noble privilege prevailed. The non-noble commissioned officers, mostly from middle-class backgrounds, faced dim prospects for promotion above the rank of captain in either the infantry or the cavalry, regardless of their talents. For instance, non-nobles composed about a third of the lieutenants and captains of infantry in the Prussian army just before the French Revolution, yet in 1789 only two non-nobles were found among the infantry's 379 majors, lieutenant-colonels, and colonels. The situation was much the same in the infantry and cavalry branches of other armies. A non-noble officer's prospects for promotion were slightly better in the artillery and engineers, branches in which he might expect to reach the rank of major over a long career.

Two other social-political impediments to military efficiency in the Neo-

classical age were the tendencies of noble officers to look on their com-
missions as privileges of their class and monarchs to oblige them by creating
officer positions out of proportion to the army's need. These tendencies
were less true of the Prussian army, in which military efficiency was more
highly prized than in other armies, but unneeded officer positions proliferated in most armies in response to noble demand. Perhaps the French
army was the worst offender in this respect. On the eve of the War of the
Austrian Succession (1740–1748), it had an officer for every eleven enlisted
men; on the eve of the Seven Years' War (1756–1763) a general for every
forty enlisted men; and on the eve of the French Revolution, it had 1,156
generals and about 10,000 other officers (two-thirds of them noble) for
174,000 troops (one officer for approximately every sixteen enlisted men).
True, many of these excess officers were on extended leave and amounted
to a reserve which could make expansion of the army easier in wartime,
but their number was out of proportion to any likely need.

Britain's royal army had different problems from those on the continent.
The army was relatively small (even on the eve of the American Revolution
in 1775 it numbered only about 50,000 men) and the officer corps, composed
mostly of the landed gentry, was correspondingly intimate. Under the
purchase system, an officer at the entry level in the infantry or cavalry
bought his commission in a particular regiment, and upon each promotion
through the rank of colonel he was required to buy a new commission. If
he could not afford the commission of the next higher rank when offered,
he might be stuck in the lower officer grades for the rest of his career. On
the other hand, if he was finally promoted into the ranks of the general
officers, he kept his colonel's commission and pay in his old regiment and,
in addition, received a general's stipend and sometimes special monetary
rewards. In his absence, the regiment was commanded by the lieutenant-
colonel. In peacetime at least, personal wealth or a wealthy patron counted
for more than sheer talent.

The enlisted ranks of eighteenth-century armies were filled with men on
the opposite end of the social scale from the commissioned officers and
included landless peasants, urban poor, and vagrants. Some common soldiers had voluntarily enlisted because they lacked better prospects in civilian life, others because they were the victims of the press gang. As a
group, they were no more representative of a cross section of the manpower
of the country than the commissioned officers. An enlisted man might reach
the non-commissioned ranks of corporal or sergeant, but it was rare for
one to cross the social gulf to become a commissioned officer. The obligated
service of the enlisted man was always long—seven years the minimum
term and fifteen years typical—and serfs conscripted into the Austrian and
Russian armies might serve twenty-five years to life. Enlisted men received
meagre pay, sometimes suffered punishments such as flogging, spent most
of their time drilling, and led a generally spartan life relieved by drink and

gambling. Yet such soldiers should not be dismissed too lightly; some fought with great valor, and some royal units had surprisingly good *esprit de corps*.

### B. Technology, Tactics and Logistics

The muzzle-loading rifled musket or rifle (a musket with spirals cut inside the barrel so as to impart a spin on the ball for better range and accuracy) had been invented at least by the seventeenth century, but in the eighteenth century a rifle cost about four times as much as a smoothbore musket and was too expensive for general issue. Also, the resistance of rifling to the ball during loading reduced the rifled musket's rate of fire to about half that of a smoothbore. Accordingly, in the Neoclassical age only special units intended for skirmishing and sniping—light infantry such as the German *Jaeger*—were armed with rifled shoulder arms. Some American frontiersmen armed with "Kentucky long rifles" (actually Pennsylvania long rifles) functioned as light infantry during the colonial wars, and during the American Revolution they could sometimes hit man-sized targets at three times the distance possible with the smoothbore musket. But such riflemen were vulnerable while reloading, they were relatively few in number compared to the infantry of the line, and the muzzle-loading rifle remained the tool of the specialist until well into the nineteenth century.

The infantry regiment was the basic building block of armies in the Neoclassical age, and in battle each continental European regiment usually deployed in two battalions, typically numbering about eight hundred men apiece. British regiments were usually about a thousand men at full strength, though in some cases, as during the American Revolution, a British regiment was so small that it could deploy only a single battalion of about five hundred men. Toward the end of the period, a typical European infantry battalion consisted of six companies of the line and two flank companies. One flank company was composed of grenadiers, usually the largest men in the regiment, and, despite their brimless mitre-like headgear, they were no longer grenade throwers but specialists at shock action with the bayonet. The other flank company was composed of light infantry, usually smaller, agile men who were specially trained for detached duties and fighting as skirmishers. The flank companies of several battalions were sometimes formed together for special missions. Grenadiers and light infantry composed the British task force of about eight hundred men sent out from Boston in April 1775 to seize an arms cache at Concord and whose clash with American militia at Lexington set off the War of the American Revolution.

On the battlefields of continental Europe, the infantry battalion normally formed in three ranks, sometimes behind a screen of skirmishers provided by a company of light infantry. Allowing for short intervals between companies and platoons (subdivisions of the company), a battalion had a typical frontage of 150–200 yards and a depth of about nine yards. Frequently, an army deployed its infantry battalions in two lines, the second about three hundred paces behind the first, in order to absorb enemy breakthroughs and to provide a reserve. The frontage occupied by a deployed army varied with its size and the density of its deployment. For instance, at the Battle of Leuthen in 1757, an Austrian army of 80,000 men occupied a front of five miles, but the more typical battle front was two to three miles in length. In any case, from high ground a commanding general could often see his whole army and that of the enemy.

The deployment of artillery on the battlefield was regulated according to the linear deployment of the infantry. The lighter field guns were usually grouped in batteries of two to six pieces and scattered among the intervals between infantry battalions. The heavier pieces were often concentrated before the center of the army's battle line. Except for horse artillery (composed of light six-pounders whose gunners rode the limbers, an innovation introduced by Frederick the Great), draft animals driven by civilian drivers dragged the guns into position before battle, the gunners walking beside them. The teamsters then withdrew their animals to the safety of the army's wagon trains in the distant rear. Except for guns small enough to be man-handled (such as Frederick's six-pounder and a four-pounder), artillery remained immobile during battle.

Though cavalry remained important, the proportion of horsemen to foot soldiers declined from as many as a fourth of an army early in the eighteenth century to as little as a seventh by its middle. This decline was probably caused in part by the increase of the infantry's firepower following the adoption of the musket and socket-bayonet combination. It was also partly due to the growth in the size of the supply trains, and, therefore, an increased competition for fodder by the draft animals (usually horses and mules) which drew the carts and wagons. Each cavalry mount and draft animal consumed a minimum of twenty pounds of fodder per day, and beyond seventy miles (or a five-day march) from the nearest magazine, fodder had to be supplied at least in part from local forage. Despite the problems of feeding the horses of the cavalry, mounted soldiers remained necessary for reconnaissance, protecting the flanks of the army on the battlefield, delivering charges against broken infantry, and, of course, attacking and counterattacking opposing cavalry.

With armies so similar in social-political character, technology, organization, and logistics, even relatively slight technical and organizational improvements were of importance. Prussia's infantry gained a significant edge in firepower over rival infantry when their wooden ramrods were replaced with iron ramrods and their muskets were redesigned with funnel-shaped touch holes. The iron ramrod allowed the Prussian infantryman to drive his charge home energetically without fear of warping or breaking the ramrod, while the funnel-shaped touch hole allowed powder from the cartridge to spill automatically into the priming pan, eliminating the need for a separate procedure for priming. These technical improvements were partly responsible for the ability of Prussian infantry battalions to fire three volleys, and sometimes four, in the time it took an opposing battalion to fire two. Similarly, the Prussian infantry's adoption of the quick step (120 paces a minute), when other infantry still marched at ninety paces a minute, allowed the Prussian infantry battalions to maneuver on the battlefield more rapidly than their opponents.

King Frederick-William I (r. 1713–1740) was responsible for the special emphasis on close-order drill in the Prussian infantry, and he has been compared with Philip of Macedon who created the army that his son Alexander the Great made famous in the ancient world. But whereas Philip was a distinguished campaigner in his own right and possessed a well-balanced army, Frederick-William I never led his army to war, and his chief military legacy to his son Frederick II (the Great) in 1740 was a superbly drilled infantry. The army was weak in artillery and cavalry, shortcomings that Frederick II had to remedy during and after the War of the Austrian Succession (1740–1748). But in the Seven Years' War (1756–1763), an improved Prussian army often stood between Prussia and disaster, and the war was also the one in which Frederick's generalship was at its best.

## II. The European Navies in the Neoclassical Age

### A. The British Navy

In the Neoclassical age, Britain was first among the world's sea powers, followed by France, Spain, and Holland. By 1775 the British empire had matured from a loose system of chartered companies, colonies, and overseas bases into an organized mercantilistic network held together by the British navy. With Britain as Europe's leading sea power, it is not surprising that her overseas empire was more secure in time of war, and therefore more capable of flourishing and even expanding, than any other. And the wealth of the British empire helped to make the home country prosperous and able to bear the expense of a superior fleet. On the other hand, as the events of the War of the American Revolution were to prove, Britain was not invulnerable if its North American colonies rebelled and enough European naval powers ganged against it. Though Britain mobilized 123 ships of the line in that conflict, the Franco-Spanish-Dutch coalition against Britain eventually mobilized 160 ships of the line.

Another limiting factor on Britain's sea power in the Neoclassical age was the long time in which the influence of formalism hobbled British tactical doctrine. The growth of formalism commenced during the War of the Spanish Succession, when, in 1703, Admiral George Rooke issued fighting instructions to his fleet that imposed a strict line-ahead formation during battle. The influence of formalism was increased with Rooke's victory at the Battle of Malaga (1707) in which the admiral adhered to the policy of a closely-controlled line while fending off an enemy fleet attempting to support a recapture of Gibraltar. The real damage was done, however, when Rooke's instructions were made the basis of the *Permanent Fighting Instructions* (PFI) issued by the admiralty in 1713. The PFI called for the British fleet to form in the weather gauge and to engage the enemy only in conterminous line (van-to-van, center-to-center, rear-to-rear, or, in some circumstances, in reverse). All flag signals were keyed to articles in the PFI, and the clumsy system made it hard for an admiral to convey special instructions to his subordinates or to depart from approved doctrine regardless of circumstance.

At least two British admirals, the so-called "Unfortunates," were victims of the PFI. Thomas Mathews was court-martialed and cashiered from the service in 1744 for his defeat while improperly engaging a French fleet in the Mediterranean when the alternative would have been to allow it to slip into port. The admiralty must have felt some guilt in Mathews's case, for afterwards it introduced Article 25 (General Chase) which provided that "when the enemy be put to the run," a British admiral might engage the enemy in other than conterminous line. The article was successfully exploited by admirals George Anson and Edward Hawke in the two successive battles at Cape Finisterre in 1747, and perhaps the failure of Admiral John Byng, the second of the Unfortunates, to exploit the article in 1756 under different circumstances was his undoing.

At the outbreak of the Seven Years' War in 1756, Byng was commanding the British Mediterranean fleet based at Gibraltar. Before Byng could shift his fleet to Port Mahon on Minorca, he learned that the French had landed forces on the island and placed the British garrison at the port under siege. Byng's fleet sailed to the garrison's relief, but, upon arrival off Port Mahon, found a French fleet barring the way. Byng then botched an attempt to engage the French fleet in conterminous line by approaching it at too sharp an angle, the French fleet crossing the "T" and heavily damaging the ships in Byng's van. But Byng's fatal error was in not using Article 25 to release his other ships to come to the assistance of the battered van and then concluding that his reformed line was too weak to continue the engagement. His fleet sailed back to Gibraltar and the British garrison at Port Mahon was compelled to surrender. Byng had "gone by the book" in all his actions, but following the rules did not save him from the consequences of the public outcry at his failure. The admiralty was pressured into convening a court-martial, and, though Byng was cleared of the charge of cowardice, he was found guilty of failing to do his utmost to defeat the enemy, a capital offense. After George II refused to pardon Byng, the unfortunate admiral was executed by firing squad.

In the aftermath of the Byng Affair, the grip of the PFI on British admirals was somewhat weakened, but for many years afterwards their conduct in battle varied greatly according to individual personalities and willingness to take risks. In 1759 Admiral Edward Boscawen used "General Chase" to attack and defeat a French fleet sheltering in the Bay of Lagos on the Portuguese coast, and in the same year Hawke also used Article 25 to make a successful attack on a French fleet anchored in Quiberon Bay. Obviously, neither enemy fleet had been "put to the run" before the British admiral in each case released his ships from the line, but the British admiralty did not question the tactics of successful admirals.

That the PFI continued to inhibit and confuse British admirals was amply illustrated at the crucial battle of Virginia Capes (or Cape Henry) near the close of the American Revolution in September 1781 when the sea communications of the British army at Yorktown were hanging in the balance. Admiral Sir Thomas Graves's fleet of nineteen of the line was outnumbered by a French fleet of twenty-four of the line under Admiral Comte de Grasse, but the fatal difficulty for the British proved to be in signals. Graves tried to engage the French fleet in conterminous line as provided in the PFI but ended up with his fleet at such an angle to the French that his rear division under Samuel Hood remained out of range. As Graves used the PFI to signal Hood to "maintain line-ahead" but also to "engage the enemy more closely," his orders seemed contradictory. Hood's decision to keep his division in line and out of range of the enemy contributed to Graves's subsequent defeat and the retreat of his fleet to New York. In consequence, and in the deciding event of the war, the British army at Yorktown, trapped by a Franco-American army, was forced to surrender in October.

In the aftermath of the American Revolution, the British admiralty abandoned formalism, developed a more flexible system of signals, and, on the eve of the British entry into the Wars of the French Revolution and Napoleon, issued fighting instructions that allowed British admirals a much wider degree of discretion in choosing tactics. These measures cleared the way for admirals such as Horatio Nelson to exercise their talents freely and were in part responsible for some of the greatest British victories ever achieved under sail, including Nelson's famous victories over the French at the Nile (1798), over the Danes at Copenhagen (1801), and over a combined Franco-Spanish fleet at Trafalgar (1805).

## B. Improvements in the Neoclassical Navies

In their essentials, sailing warships changed relatively little in the Neoclassical period, but a few refinements were introduced. Copper sheeting of the underwater hulls helped to discourage marine life from attaching itself and reducing speed and damaging wood. Toward the end of the eighteenth century, flintlock ignition replaced slow matches for firing guns, and the British invented the carronade, a large-caliber but short-ranged sixty-four pounder, useful for close-fought actions. The rear wheels on gun trucks were also made adjustable so that a gun could fire at an angle from its port. A major step forward in navigation took place when a reliable marine chronometer appeared in 1765, something essential to determining accurate longitude with a sextant. Beginning in 1768, the British captain James Cook successfully relied on the improved means of navigation while carrying out a series of exploratory voyages that took him to such distant points in the Pacific ocean as Tahiti, New Zealand, Australia, Antarctica, and the Hawaiian islands.

Long-range voyaging also benefitted from progress against disease. James Lind, a British naval surgeon, carried out a study of the possible treatments for the dreaded scourge of scurvy, known today to be caused by dietary deficiency of vitamin C. By 1754 Lind's experiments convinced him that citrus juice was an effective antiscorbutic, and Cook proved Lind's contention when he issued lemon juice regularly to his crews during his voyage of 1772 and lost not a man to either scurvy or dysentery. Lind also linked dirty clothes and hammocks to disease, and late in the century the British navy began the practice of washing recruits and issuing them clean clothes and hammocks. Greater attention to hygiene, along with the regular use of antiscorbutics, reduced the number of yearly sick in the British navy from 38% in 1780 to 7% in 1805. On the other hand, the problems of bad water and bad food were never really solved in the Age of Sail. The issue of "grog" (a mixture of rum and water) to make bad water more palatable resulted in the high rate of alcoholism that probably contributed to more men being killed in the British navy from falls from the tops than in battle. Nor was a steady diet of salted pork and sea biscuit conducive to longevity among sailors.

Naval officer training became only marginally more formalized as the eighteenth century wore on. Britain established a naval academy at Portsmouth-Gosport in 1733 (the Royal Naval College as of 1806), and France established the Marine Academy in 1752. But tuition at these institutions was not free and the great majority of officer-candidates continued to learn their duties as midshipmen aboard ship, some of them starting out as young as age twelve. In the British navy, a midshipman might offer himself for examination for promotion to lieutenant after six years at sea, two of which had to be served as a passed midshipman or ensign. His further promotion through the rank of captain came by selection and was usually rapid or not at all. Promotion in the admiral ranks was usually by seniority. Still, the lack of an aristocratic background was less of a hindrance to a British naval officer than to the officers in some of the other European navies.

## III. European Wars of the Neoclassical Age

### A. The War of the Austrian Succession, 1740–1748

The death of the Austrian Habsburg emperor Charles VI in October 1740 and the succession of his daughter Maria Theresa to his throne though the

Pragmatic Sanction set off attempts by other European powers to partition the Austrian empire. Frederick II of Prussia commenced hostilities when he ordered his army to invade Silesia in December 1740, and the war accelerated in 1741 when Maria Theresa found herself also at war with Louis XV of France, Philip V of Spain, and Charles Albert, Elector of Bavaria. But Maria Theresa's enemies underestimated the loyalty of her subjects, the fitness of her army, and the willingness of other powers to intervene on Austria's behalf. In particular, from the time of Queen Anne's death in 1714 and the succession of her cousin George, Elector of Hanover, to the British throne as George I (r. 1714–1727), Britain had been deeply involved in German affairs. As Elector of Hanover as well as King of Great Britain, George II (r. 1727–1760) was especially jealous of his Hanoverian patrimony.

In 1740 Frederick II had just arrived to the Prussian throne and was only twenty-eight years old. Thus, the war over Silesia offered him a practical course in generalship, though not one without painful lessons. At the Battle of Moellwitz in April 1741, the superior Austrian cavalry drove the Prussian cavalry from the field and seemed so near to inflicting a total defeat on the Prussian army that Frederick took refuge in flight. Fortunately for the young king, Field Marshal Kurt von Schwerin remained behind to rally the Prussian army and to lead it to victory. The embarrassed Frederick was twenty miles away from the field when he learned of Schwerin's success. Still,

Central Europe and the Campaigns of Frederick the Great, 1740 - 1763

Frederick was inspired to strengthen his cavalry, and this effort was rewarded in the spring of 1742 when, during the Prussian invasion of Bohemia, his mounted arm clinched his victory over the Austrians at the Battle of Chotusitz. Soon after, Maria Theresa recognized Frederick's conquest of Silesia, and Prussia left the war.

The Austrian army's performance against the French and Bavarians was more impressive than its performance against the Prussian army, and before the middle of 1743 Austrian troops had driven the Franco-Bavarian forces from Bohemia, Austria, and Bavaria. Matters worsened for France when the Pragmatic Army (so-called for its support of the Pragmatic Sanction) assembled on the Lower Rhine. Composed of 40,000 British, German, and Dutch troops, the Pragmatic Army was under the personal command of George II of Great Britain. It marched up the Rhine in order to aid the Austrians in much the same fashion as the Duke of Marlborough's army had come to the aid of the Austrians four decades earlier, but George II was no Marlborough. A French army of 37,000 troops nearly trapped his army in the valley of the river Main near Dettigen in late June 1743, and only by dint of hard fighting did the Pragmatic Army extract itself from a near-disaster. George II did not lack courage, and his personal leadership of his infantry in a counterattack against French cavalry during the battle is still a famous episode in British history. Yet Dettigen turned out to be the last battle in which a British monarch commanded in the field, and, after the Pragmatic Army returned to the defense of the Austrian Netherlands (Belgium), its command passed to William Augustus, Duke of Cumberland and third son of George II.

Cumberland's mettle as a general was tested in the spring of 1745 when Louis XV and a French army of 70,000 troops under Marshal Maurice de Saxe invaded the Austrian Netherlands. One of the finest generals of the age, Saxe left 20,000 men to besiege Tournai and ordered the rest of his army to fortify a position at Fontenoy in order to block any attempt at relief by the Pragmatic Army, by then a force of 50,000 troops. In the Battle of Fontenoy in May, made famous for, among other reasons, the punctilio observed before action (officers of the British Grenadier Guards exchanged toasts with the officers of the French Guard across the battlefield), Cumberland's army penetrated the first line of French earthworks and even imperiled Louis XV with the threat of capture. Saxe, so ill that he had to command from a litter, managed to launch the troops of his second line in a counterattack that finally forced Cumberland to withdraw his army from the field. After his victory at Fontenoy, Saxe went on to capture Tournai, and by the end of summer his army had also seized Ghent, Bruges, Oudenarde, Ostend, and Brussels.

In the summer of 1744 Prussia reentered the war as an ally of France, and during 1745 Frederick II reached the peak of his form as a general in the War of the Austrian Succession. After an Austrian army of 80,000 men invaded Silesia in June, Frederick's outnumbered army marched all night in order to launch an attack at dawn on the enemy's camp at Hohenfried-burg. The surprised Austrians were defeated and driven back into Bohemia. At the end of September Prince Charles of Lorraine, the Austrian com-mander, took a leaf from Frederick's book by carrying out a night march that placed the Austrian army near Sohr in the Prussian rear. Before the Austrians could attack, Frederick detected the danger, caused his army to wheel about, and then launched an attack that opened up a line of retreat into Silesia. Once on Silesian soil, Frederick's forces defeated all Austrian attempts to invade, and Maria Theresa's representatives made peace with Frederick on Christmas Day.

The rest of the War of the Austrian Succession was anti-climactic. Saxe's army penetrated the Dutch Netherlands and captured Maastricht in 1747, but the arrival of a Russian army on the Rhine posed a threat to eastern France. Moreover, the Spanish were not very successful in their campaigns against the Austrians in northern Italy. Peace negotiations were prolonged, but the Treaty of Aix-la-Chapelle (October 1748) restored Dutch territory, left Silesia to Prussia, Hanover to George II, and, except for some minor territories in northern Italy, guaranteed the rest of Maria Theresa's legacy.

The War of the Austrian Succession was the background for the "Rising of the '45," the last major civil war on the island of Britain. With the aid of France, and while George II's government was preoccupied with the war on the continent, Prince Charles Edward Stuart ("Bonnie Prince Char-lie" or the "Young Pretender") landed in the Hebrides in August 1745 and raised an army from the highland clans of Scotland and other Jacobin fac-tions. The Stuart army seized Edinburgh in September and subsequently invaded northern England to capture Carlisle, Manchester, and Derby. But the return of the Duke of Cumberland with troops from the continent compelled Charles to withdraw his army deep inside Scotland, and the issue was finally decided at the Battle of Culloden Moor, northeast of In-verness, in April 1746.

In the Battle of Culloden, Cumberland had 9,000 well-armed, well-trained troops, while Charles possessed only a ragged army of about 5,000 men, many of them armed only with swords and crude pikes. Charles ruined what little chance for victory he may have had by allowing Cumberland's artillery ample opportunity to hammer his army's ranks, and it was finally too weak to prevail over the fire of Cumberland's infantry or the attack of its cavalry. Charles survived the defeat at Culloden to escape to France, but 2,000 of his supporters had lost their lives. As half the dead were dispatched while lying wounded or after being taken prisoner, the episode gives lie to the notion that Neoclassical warfare, however formal, was nec-essarily kinder or more limited than any other.

## B. The Seven Years' War, 1756–1763

The origins of the Seven Years' War lay in a so-called diplomatic revo-lution in Europe between 1748 and 1756. Maria Theresa was never reconciled to her loss of Silesia, yet doubted the ability of Austria alone to recover it in war. Moreover, Prussia's emergence as a great power in Germany had disturbed French and Russian calculations. Accordingly, an alliance among Austria, France, and Russia was formed against Prussia to reduce its power and territory to the point of inconsequence. The government of George II—fearful for the balance of power, the safety of the dynastic dependency of Hanover, and already unofficially at war with Louis XV in North America—made an alliance with Frederick II. Britain promised Frederick financial subsidies, naval operations against France, and 40,000 troops to help in the defense of Hanover. Frederick's army numbered 186,000 well-trained and well-equipped troops. Even so, Prussia faced long odds.

Frederick's original strategy was to defeat Austria and its allies in the German states before France and Russia could fully mobilize their forces, but his early campaigns proved indecisive and by the fall of 1757 Prussia was in great peril. An Austrian army under Marshal Daun invaded Silesia, a Franco-Austrian army under the Duke of Soubise advanced on western Prussia, and a Russian army under Marshal Stepan Apraksin moved into eastern Prussia. In these circumstances, Frederick placed his hopes for survival on a "hold-and-strike" strategy. He used most of his forces and his fortresses to delay the advance of two of the invading armies, and, with the remainder of his army under his personal command, struck at the third.

Frederick's strategy was first rewarded at the Battle of Rossbach in early November 1757 when his army of 21,000 men faced the 64,000 men of Soubise's army. With a three-to-one advantage in troops, Soubise tried to turn the flank of the Prussian army, but his overconfidence was his undoing. A sudden Prussian cavalry charge led by General Friedrich von Seydlitz smashed into the French ranks while still in marching order, and, after Prussian infantry and artillery joined in Seydlitz's attack, Frederick's army won the battle in only an hour and a half of fighting. Of Soubise's troops, 8,000 were casualties on the field and 20,000 deserted. Frederick's losses came to fewer than six hundred men.

After his victory at Rossbach, Frederick gathered reinforcements to increase his army's strength to 36,000 men and marched over two hundred miles in order to confront 80,000 Austrian troops under Marshal Daun at Leuthen in early December. When his army deployed from marching order into battle order, Frederick introduced his so-called Oblique Maneuver. In this deployment, some of his battalions were concealed behind a line of hills at an angle to the end of the enemy's line. While the Austrians were preoccupied with the Prussian threat to their front, these battalions launched an attack that took the Austrian army in the flank and began to roll up its line. Daun's counterattack with cavalry came too late, and by the end of the day the Austrian army was in retreat after losing 20,000 men. Frederick's losses came to 6,500 troops. After the Austrians retreated into Bohemia, Frederick marched against the Russians, but they withdrew from Prussian territory without offering battle. Perhaps Frederick's campaign of 1757 was the most brilliant in his long career.

In 1758 a Russian army of 50,000 troops invaded Prussia and laid siege to the fortress of Kuestrin on the river Oder. In August Frederick led 36,000 troops to Kuestrin's relief, crossing the Oder some distance from Kuestrin in order to sever Russian communications. When the Russian army turned back to deal with this threat it found itself trapped between the confluence of two rivers near Zorndorff. Then occurred perhaps the bloodiest battle of the Neoclassical age, as Frederick launched attack after attack against the Russian lines and, with equal determination, the Russians repelled each attack in turn. By nightfall the battle had ended in a draw but half the Russians and 14,000 of Frederick's soldiers were casualties. Frederick was so appalled at the carnage that the next day he prudently allowed the surviving Russians to withdraw unmolested.

By 1759 Frederick had lost 100,000 of the troops with whom he had begun the war, many of them, as in the opposing armies, to disease and exposure. New soldiers brought his army's strength to 150,000 men, but they did not compare in training and discipline to the men he had lost. Moreover, he had scant means to protect Hanover. Fortunately for George II, an Anglo-German army of 45,000 troops commanded by Ferdinand, Duke of Brunswick, was able to win a memorable victory at the Battle of Minden over a French army of 60,000 men in August 1759. In this action, the British infantry brigade distinguished itself by first beating off a French cavalry charge and then charging the enemy with such impressive discipline and gallantry that, despite heavy losses (of 4,434 men engaged, 1,330 were casualties), it broke a hole in the French line. Brunswick ordered cavalry under General George, Lord Sackville, to attack through the gap, but, for reasons never satisfactorily explained, Sackville failed to obey. The French took the opportunity to retire from the field in good order. Though Sackville was court-martialed and discharged from the army for his failure to act at Minden, he would commit a much worse blunder fewer that twenty years later. As Lord Germain and secretary of state for war and the colonies during the American Revolution, his failure to coordinate British operations in 1777 contributed to General John Burgoyne's defeat at Saratoga, the turning point of the war.

In the month that Minden was fought, Frederick and 50,000 Prussian troops engaged an Austro-Russian army of 90,000 men under Count Peter Soltikov and Marshal Daun at the Battle of Kunnersdorff near the Oder, and, because of poorly coordinated attacks, Frederick lost about 20,000 men and 178 guns in six hours of fighting. So great was Frederick's defeat that during the subsequent retreat the Prussian king contemplated abdication and even suicide. His confidence returned when his army was joined by troops from Brunswick's army, but his cause seemed to be living on borrowed time. In August 1760, his army barely avoided encirclement in the Battle of Liegnitz, and in October it was unable to prevent an Austro-

Russian raid from burning Berlin, his capital. At the Battle of Torgau in November, Marshal Daun was on the point of inflicting another "Kunnersdorff" on Frederick when a Prussian cavalry attack barely saved the day. A nearly destitute Prussian king led his dwindling army against his enemies in 1761, and, as the end of the year approached, it seemed that only a miracle could save Prussia from final defeat.

Amazingly, the miracle came to pass. The Tsarina Elizabeth died, and Tsar Peter III, her successor and an avowed admirer of Frederick, withdrew Russia from the alliance against Frederick and even loaned him troops to serve against his enemies. In the summer of 1762 Peter was deposed in a coup and was succeeded by Tsarina Catherine II (the Great), but, although she withdrew aid to Frederick, she did not bring Russia back into the war. In July 1762 the revived Prussian army defeated Marshal Daun's forces at the Battle of Burkersdorff, in November Brunswick's army drove the French army back across the Rhine, and in February 1763 the Peace of Huburtusburg left Prussia intact. But the harrowing experience of the Seven Years' War left its mark on Frederick; though he engineered the First Partition of Poland in 1772, it was bloodless, and, except for a show of force against Austria in 1778 in a quarrel over Bavaria, he never led his army into the field again until his death in August 1786.

## IV. The Neoclassical Wars Overseas

### A. The Struggles for India

By the eighteenth century the British East India Trading Company had numerous stations and forts in India, the most important being at Madras, Calcutta, and Bombay. The greatest of the Company's European rivals in India were the French who had founded their first station in Carnatic at Pondicherry, 150 miles south of Madras, in 1673. The British and French restrained their rivalries as long as the Mogul empire was intact, but in 1739 the empire received a fatal blow when a Persian-Afghan invasion sacked the Grand Mogul's capital at Delhi, and the rajahs and nawabs, princes who ruled much of India in the name of the Great Mogul, asserted their independence and began to fight among themselves for power and position. In order to safeguard their interests amidst growing chaos, the British and French took sides among the Indian factions and became rivals for control of India.

The breakdown of the Mogul empire and the French threat convinced the Company's directors in London that only Company troops trained and equipped to European standards could safeguard their positions in India. The directors employed John Stringer Lawrence, a retired British captain and a veteran of the Battle of Culloden, to turn the heterogeneous collection of policemen and warehouse guards at Madras into a proper Company

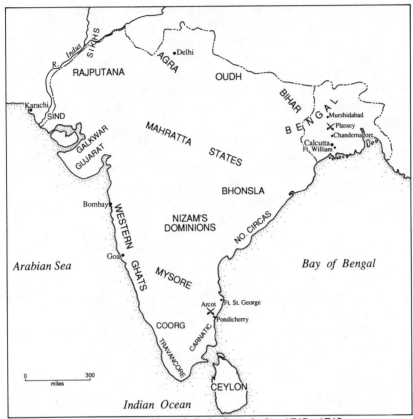

Expansion of British Rule Over India, 1745 - 1763

regiment. Robert Clive, a Company clerk, was appointed as Lawrence's assistant. Lawrence proceeded to found a European battalion consisting of seven companies (each company was composed of three commissioned officers, four sergeants, four corporals, three drummers, and seventy privates), and a *sepoy* or Indian battalion organized along the same lines. The two battalions constituted the Madras regiment, the cornerstone of a Company army that, before the century was over, numbered 150,000 men.

Lawrence returned to England after founding the regiment at Madras, and in his absence a power struggle broke out among the Indian princes of Carnatic in 1748. When the French at Pondicherry supported Chunda Sahib against the Company's protegé Mohammed Ali, Clive assumed command of an expedition of European and sepoy troops bent on capturing Chunda Sahib's capital at Arcot. The effort was successful, but for fifty days and nights Clive's heavily outnumbered troops had to beat off repeated attempts by Chunda Sahib's forces to recapture the place. Finally, a Mahratta prince threw his support to the Company, Lawrence returned to India in order to assume command of the Company's forces, and Chunda

Sahib was decisively defeated. The episode seemed to prove out the Company's foresight in building a regiment at Madras, but, as another prudent measure, the directors requested that George II's government send royal troops to India.

In 1754 the Thirty-Ninth Regiment of Foot (whose regimental banner would later carry the words "Primus in Indis") arrived at Madras. Its posting marked the beginning of a long association between the Company army and the British royal army that lasted down to the abolition of the East India Company after the Great Sepoy Mutiny in 1857. The arrival of the regiment came none too soon for a new crisis was brewing in Bengal. In the spring of 1756, and with encouragement from the French, Surajah Dowla, the Nizam or Viceroy of Bengal, ordered his semi-feudal army to attack the Company station at Ft. William. Unlike the British force at Ft. St. George at Madras, that at Ft. William was neither strong nor well-trained. The fort was successfully stormed by Surajah Dowla's troops in June, and, following his victory, Surajah Dowla threw 146 of his prisoners into the punishment cell of the fort. There they were so overcrowded that only twenty-three of them emerged alive the next morning. The "Black Hole of Calcutta" has remained forever famous in Anglo-Indian history.

Lawrence entrusted the task of recovering the Company's position in Bengal to Clive, who assembled an expeditionary force at Madras consisting of regulars from the Thirty-Ninth of Foot and soldiers drawn from the Madras European and Indian battalions, perhaps altogether 4,000 troops. Four British warships escorted the transports bearing the troops to the coast of Bengal and then up the Hoogly river until they arrived off Ft. William on January 1, 1757. Following a British naval bombardment, Ft. William's Indian garrison surrendered, and Clive's troops subsequently drove Surajah Dowla's forces from the vicinity. Then Clive's troops advanced a further thirty miles up the Hoogly to take the French station at Chandernagore.

However, as long as Surajah Dowla remained in power in Bengal, the Company's position there would never be secure, and, after failing to remove the Nizam by intrigue, Clive turned to force in the spring of 1757. Leaving part of his command to hold conquered territory, and with just 750 European soldiers and 2,500 sepoys, Clive advanced on Surajah Dowla's capital at Murshidabad, 120 miles from Ft. William. Upon hearing the news, Surajah Dowla put himself at the head of a semi-feudal army of 50,000 men and marched to intercept Clive's army. The two armies, the one vastly outnumbering the other, finally clashed in a decisive battle on June 23 near the village of Plassey, just south of Mangora, on the banks of the Cosimbazar river.

At the Battle of Plassey, Clive drew up his army in line, the European battalion at its center and battalions of sepoys on the wings. Surajah Dowla's forces launched repeated attacks, trying through sheer numbers to overwhelm Clives's forces, but disciplined firepower threw back each as-

sault. When the Indians wavered, Clive launched a counterattack and Surajah Dowla's army disintegrated and fled the field. The Battle of Plassey
was not particularly bloody—only about five hundred of Surajah Dowla's
troops were left dead on the battlefield, and Clive's army suffered just sixty
casualties—but it had settled the fate of Bengal and placed the British on
the road to the eventual conquest of India. In the wake of his defeat, Surajah
Dowla was assassinated at Murshidabad, and Mir Jafar, who threw in his
lot with the British, was appointed by Clive as the new Nizam of Bengal.
Clive returned to Ft. William, where he remained until 1760 when he retired
to England.

While Clive's forces were consolidating the Company's hold on Bengal,
the reduced garrison at Ft. St. George in Madras faced a threat from the
French at Pondicherry. The French station served as the base of two regular
French infantry regiments as well as that of regiments of sepoys in the pay
of the French. This formidable force advanced to impose a siege on Ft. St.
George in January 1759. The aging Lawrence rallied the defenders to repel
French attacks until February when a British fleet arrived, the siege was
raised, and the French forces fell back to Pondicherry. In 1760 General Eyre
Coote arrived at Madras with reinforcements, took the field against the
French, and decisively defeated them in the Battle of Wandewash. He then
laid siege to Pondicherry until its garrison surrendered in January 1761. By
then French power in India was virtually extinguished, and the Peace of
Paris in 1763 reduced the French presence in the sub-continent to a few
unfortified stations. In future, Britain's principal enemies in India would
be confined to native potentates.

## B. The Struggles for North America

The counterparts to the War of the Austrian Succession and the Seven
Years' War in North America were respectively King George's War and
the French and Indian War. Though the various European colonies in North
America had been caught up in earlier wars of the Old World, in none of
them had they mobilized more than 5,000 men (Indian allies included) on
a side. But almost from their foundings the English colonies had assumed
primary responsibility for their own defense, and, with the exception of
Quaker-dominated Pennsylvania, each had imposed a militia obligation on
its citizens and, in some cases, hired semi-regular provincial troops. Accordingly, the English colonies were accustomed to calling on Britain for
direct military aid only in unusual emergencies and even to paying the
expenses of regular troops sent to the colonies for as long as they remained.
Traditionally, the southern colonies were most in need of British help because of their limited white population and reluctance to arm the black
slaves on their plantations when threatened by the Indians or rival European colonies. Some of the need was removed when Georgia, founded in
1732 and the last of the original thirteen English colonies established in

NORTH AMERICA : French and Indian War, 1754 - 1763

North America, was created as both a debtors' haven and a military buffer between South Carolina and Spanish Florida.

On occasion, Britain raised provincial troops from the English colonies for her wars elsewhere. For instance, an "American Regiment" of 3,400 colonial troops was raised to participate in the British attack on Spanish Cartagena in 1740. And in 1745, on their own initiative, the colonies of New England raised 4,000 men under militia Colonel William Pepperrell for the siege and capture of the French fortress of Louisbourg on Cape Breton island at the mouth of the Gulf of St. Lawrence. The effort was the biggest American colonial military success before the American Revolution, and the New Englanders were highly chagrined when, under the terms of the Peace of Aix-la-Chapelle, Louisbourg was returned to French control.

Still, by long odds, the French and Indian War was the largest in which the original thirteen colonies participated before the American Revolution. The war had its origins in a dispute between the French and the colony of Virginia over claims to the forks of the Ohio, where the Allegheny and Monongahela rivers merge to form the mightiest river flowing east-west in eastern North America. In an age of water transportation, the Ohio was a key to settlement of the old Northwest Territories as far as the Mississippi, and the French seized the advantage when they built a log-and-earth structure they called Ft. Duquesne at the forks in 1753. After they and their Indian allies beat off an effort by troops from Virginia (led by George Washington, twenty-two-year old colonel of the militia) to expel them from the forks in 1754, Virginia's governor and colonial assembly called on Britain for help.

Though Britain issued no formal declaration of war, George II's government was determined that the French should be expelled from the forks.

Accordingly, early in 1755, General Edward Braddock and two regular regiments arrived in Virginia from Ireland to engage in the task. Braddock proceeded to assemble a regular-provincial expedition of 2,000 men (1,360 of them regulars) at Ft. Cumberland on Wills Creek for the 110-mile march to the forks. Though Washington was appointed as his provincial adviser and neither Braddock nor his officers had served before in North America, the British general paid small heed to the opinions of a young "buckskin colonel" on either tactics or logistics in mountainous and forested terrain. Instead of a fast-moving column relying on pack animals, Braddock mounted a European-style expedition encumbered by a wagon train and artillery.

Accordingly, the Anglo-American army had to build a road as it went across the rugged Allegheny mountains, averaging only two miles a day until the transit was completed early in July. Then, after leaving some of his men behind at a base camp under Colonel Thomas Dunbar, Braddock and 1,460 of his troops, including provincials under Washington, pressed on toward Ft. Duquesne. They were only three miles from the fort on July 9 when the British vanguard unexpectedly encountered 250 French troops and six hundred Indians on the narrow forest road. Though the French and Indians were as surprised as the British at the sudden head-on meeting (they were advancing to stage an ambush at a crossing of the Monongahela), they quickly recovered, took cover, and opened fire. In contrast, the red-coated British regulars tried to form a formal battle line in the forest, and thereby exposed themselves to a killing fire from a largely unseen enemy. Matters became worse when the vanguard recoiled on the main body and Braddock was mortally wounded while trying to rally his men. Panic finally seized the British soldiers and a rout ensued in the direction of Dunbar's camp. Fortunately for the survivors, the French and Indians did not pursue far, but 877 Anglo-American soldiers had been killed or wounded against a French loss of sixteen soldiers and twenty-seven Indians. When Dunbar learned of the disaster, he lost no time in organizing a retreat over the mountains.

Following the Battle of the Monongahela (or Braddock's Defeat), a full-blown French and Indian war erupted in eastern North America that lasted for years. In the early phase, the Anglo-American forces seemed so inept that the powerful Iroquois confederation, usually reliable Indian allies of the British, remained neutral and uneasy, and it was with difficulty that the British eventually wooed them into active participation. In 1757, in one of the worst episodes of the war for the Anglo-Americans, the Marquis de Montcalm, who had assumed command of the French and Indians at Ft. Ticonderoga located between Lake Champlain and Lake George, launched a raid that destroyed British Ft. William Henry, threatened the upper Hudson valley, and killed or wounded hundreds of Anglo-American settlers. Thousands more fled the frontier.

Meanwhile, the Anglo-Americans were struggling to create effective forces with which to turn the tide. As early as 1755, Governor William Shirley of Massachusetts commissioned Robert Rogers to raise a company of frontiersmen from New Hampshire for armed reconnaissance, and in 1756 the company was expanded to a battalion. Rogers's Rangers (so-called after patrols which "ranged" or patrolled between frontier outposts) dealt with the Indians on their own terms and were thoroughly familiar with the tricks of forest fighting. In imitation, Colonel Thomas Gage, who had commanded Braddock's vanguard at the battle of the Monongahela, raised a regular regiment of light infantry modeled on Rogers's Rangers. The British also raised an oversized regiment of "Royal Americans" (eventually designated as the Sixtieth Regiment of Foot) composed of 4,000 men. Still other provincial units increased the total of Americans until 20,000 had served at one time or another during the war. In addition, Britain exploited her command of the sea to ship 30,000 regular soldiers to North America. Perhaps no more than 10,000 French troops and 10,000 Indian warriors opposed these forces.

Still another improvement on the British side occurred when the statesman William Pitt in London gradually brought strategic coherence to the

Soldiers of the 6oth (Royal American) Regiment of Foot, 1755–1763. John Elting, ed., *Military Uniforms of America, 1755–1795* (San Rafael, Calif.: Presidio Press, 1974), p. 7.

British war effort in North America. In 1758 two of three offensives that he ordered were successful, the failure being that of General James Abercromby's attack on Ft. Ticonderoga with 16,000 troops (6,500 of them regulars). Montcalm successfully defended the fort with an army a quarter of the size of Abercromby's. But in July 1758, the same month in which Abercromby was defeated, a British army of 9,000 troops under generals Jeffrey Amherst and James Wolfe successfully concluded a siege of Louisbourg on Cape Breton, and, before the year was out, another army under General James Forbes had recovered the forks of the Ohio.

Forbes's campaign for the forks was, in some respects, the most difficult of the three British offensives in 1758. Whereas both Abercromby and Amherst had the advantage of being able to move their armies to their objectives by water, Forbes's army of 1,700 regulars and 5,000 provincial troops, based in Carlisle, Pennsylvania, had to hack out a road as they went across the mountain. In addition, Forbes fell prey to poor health and command of the expedition was increasingly exercised by Colonel Henry Bouquet, a native Swiss and a professional soldier, and by Washington, who commanded provincial troops in Forbes's army. The glacier-like advance was not only due to the road building, terrain, and enemy opposition but also to supply problems. There was no repetition of Braddock's Defeat, however, and Forbes's army finally arrived at the site of Ft. Duquesne on November 25 only to find that the defenders, just five hundred French and Indians, had burned the fort and fled. The Anglo-Americans built a new fort at the forks and named it in honor of Pitt. Forbes returned to Philadelphia where he died in 1759. Washington returned to Virginia to seek election to the colonial assembly, and when he went into the field again almost sixteen years later, it was to take up the post of commander in chief of the American forces in the revolution.

The French were clearly on the defensive by the beginning of 1759, and, after the fall of Louisbourg, French retention of Quebec near the mouth of the St. Lawrence river became crucial for the arrival of reinforcements and supplies from Europe. Pitt recognized this fact and appointed Wolfe to command an expedition of 9,000 regulars and 400 Rangers assembled at Louisbourg for the purpose of capturing Quebec. This force, embarked in a fleet commanded by Admiral Charles Saunders, landed on the opposite side of the St. Lawrence from Quebec in June, but Wolfe immediately discovered that the task before him was formidable. Though Montcalm's garrison numbered only 5,000 troops and militia, he commanded a fortified city whose granite walls topped cliffs towering as high as two hundred feet above the St. Lawrence river.

Wolfe's only real prospect of success lay in somehow getting British troops up the cliffs to the Plains of Abraham behind the city. Though he tried several operations against Quebec during the course of the summer of 1759, all were repelled by Montcalm's prompt countermoves. Then in September, with only a few weeks remaining before the threat of ice in the St. Lawrence would force Saunders to withdraw his fleet, Wolfe spotted a weakness in Montcalm's defenses: a lightly-guarded path leading from the Anse au Foulon (Faulon's Cove) on the river to the Plains of Abraham high above. Sending other forces to make feints elsewhere on the night of September 12–13, Wolfe managed to distract Montcalm's attention long enough for 3,500 British troops (led by Rangers and light infantry under Lieutenant-Colonel William Howe) to land at the cove, surprise and silence the guard, and steal up the path to seize a perch on the Plains of Abraham. Wolfe quickly joined Howe's men with reinforcements and soon formed 4,500 troops into a line of battle.

Once Montcalm discovered the danger, he rushed his troops to the threatened point and at mid-morning launched them in an attack on the British position. The French lines went forward bravely, but Montcalm's troops were less well-trained for fighting in the open than their British adversaries, and they wasted their early volleys at too great a range. The British regulars held their fire until the enemy was only sixty yards away, then fired volleys that tore out the center of the French line. A British charge with the bayonet completed the French defeat. But Wolfe was mortally wounded on the field, and Montcalm, injured during the retreat into Quebec, died the next day. His garrison finally surrendered Quebec on September 17.

The final campaigns of the war against the French were anticlimactic, but the most important resulted in Amherst's capture of Montreal in September 1760 and the French governor's subsequent surrender of the remaining French posts in Canada. But the Indians continued to wage war. A fierce Cherokee uprising in the Carolinas in 1761 took Ft. Loudoun (in what is now Tennessee) and massacred part of its garrison, and regular-provincial forces were not able to bring the Cherokees into submission until December. The war on the frontier in the Old Northwest continued even after the Peace of Paris was made in early 1763. That spring, Pontiac, chief of the Ottawas, led a general Indian uprising that overwhelmed every British post west of Ft. Niagara except Ft. Detroit and Ft. Pitt. The siege of the latter was raised when Colonel Bouquet's regulars won the bloody Battle of Bushy Run in August, a reflection of how far the British army had come since Braddock's time. Ft. Detroit was relieved in November. Sporadic fighting continued with the Indians, however, until a formal peace was made with them in July 1766, exactly ten years before the American Declaration of Independence.

## V. The Legacies of the Neoclassical Age

### A. The American Revolution, 1775–1783

Though 2.5 million people lived in the original thirteen colonies by 1775 (about 9 million lived in the British Isles), half a million of the American population were black slaves and about an equal number were whites loyal to Britain. Perhaps a third of the 1.5 million "patriot" population were males, but probably no more than about 100,000 of them served at any time during the war, and no more than 35,000 at one time.

Though it may be thought that the war's successful outcome for the Americans represented a triumph of the New World's patterns of war over those of the Old World, in reality the Americans borrowed much (in several senses of the term) from the Old World in order to win. A knowledge of formal tactics under some conditions was vital, and the Continental Army did not begin to approach the effectiveness of British regulars on the battlefield until Friedrich Steuben, a retired major from the Prussian army of Frederick the Great and eventually the American inspector-general and drillmaster, took the infantry in hand at Valley Forge in the winter of 1777–1778. The Continentals learned linear tactics in order to be able to fight in open terrain (the infantry usually fought in two lines instead of three), to use the bayonet, and to maneuver in close formation. The militia, less well-trained, usually fought well only from behind earthworks or in wooded or broken terrain and were generally more effective against loyalist militia than against regular troops. As the war went on, the Americans also enjoyed extensive aid from France, Louis XVI's monarchy eventually providing naval support, weapons, uniforms and equipment, and ninety per cent of the American gunpowder supply.

The greatest American victory of the war without the direct involvement of other powers was Saratoga (1777), one in which an American army of about 20,000 men captured a British army of 5,800 men in backwoods New York. But perhaps even more important was the formal French entry as an American ally in February 1778. For their own reasons, Spain in 1779 and Holland in 1780 also entered the war against Britain, and the British also faced a revolt in India. The alliance with royal France was especially critical to American success. At the siege of Yorktown in 1781, the deciding event of the war, 6,500 British troops were compelled to surrender to an allied force under Washington which consisted of 9,500 American troops (3,500 of them militia), 7,800 French troops, and 15,000 French sailors and marines. The siege was carried out in Neoclassical fashion, and, indeed, Britain's defeat in the Revolution may be seen as due in part to the efforts of a coalition of Neoclassical powers opposed to her.

### B. *The Wars of the French Revolution and Napoleon, 1792–1815*

The legacies of the Neoclassical period are even clearer when the Wars of the French Revolution and Napoleon are examined. The Revolution of 1789 swept away the old class barriers in the French army and navy as in every other aspect of French life. When in 1793 the revolution imposed a *levée en masse* on a population of 25 million, the second-largest in Europe, it insured that the wartime army would be a mass army. By the end of 1794 the general draft had raised the army's strength to a million men, probably the largest in history to that time. In addition, the French revolutionary army was powerfully motivated by a sense of nationalism and patriotism lacking in the old-style royal armies. But the victories of the French in the Wars of the French Revolution (1792–1802) and the Napoleonic Wars (1803–1815) were not purely due to numbers and enthusiasm. For success, the French drew heavily from the store of ideas and developments in the army of the *ancien régime*.

In the area of infantry tactics, for example, some French officers of the old army had been dissatisfied with linear tactics because of the difficulty of maneuvering on the battlefield in long lines and because they wished to take greater advantage of light infantry as skirmishers. On maneuvers following the Seven Years' War, the French conducted experiments with advancing battalions in columns-of-divisions (the six or more companies of the battalion, one behind the next with short intervals or divisions between), the conclusions from such experiments being reflected in Colonel Jacques de Guibert's treatise *Essai général de la tactique* (1772). Guibert argued in favor of keeping the infantry battalions in columns-of-divisions (inherently maneuver formations) until nearly in range of the enemy, and then, using a drill of his devising, forming the companies quickly into line for firing. Other officers recognized in the column-of-divisions an ideal formation for shock action with the bayonet. For either purpose, clouds of skirmishers composed of light infantry could screen the French colums-of-divisions while approaching the enemy line. French infantry tactics during the Revolutionary and Napoleonic wars drew much of their inspiration from such tactical ideas of reformers in the old army.

In the realm of artillery, the French army had taken the lead after the Seven Years' War. Jean Gribeauval, inspector-general between 1760 and 1789, brought the smooth-bore field gun to a new peak of effectiveness by causing the redesign of gun carriages and the casting of barrels to reduce weight. By 1789 the French twelve pounder was a model of mobility combined with firepower, and the French army had the largest number of field guns of any army in Europe. In addition, the artillery school at Auxonne, directed by the Baron du Teil, pioneered new artillery tactics, emphasizing in its teachings the rapid massing of guns on the battlefield and the blasting of gaps in the opposing line. Young Lieutenant Napoleon Bonaparte (1769–1821) was studying at the artillery school at the outbreak of the revolution, and, as a general, his artillery methods never varied greatly from those he had learned at Auxonne. Perhaps his greatest personal contribution to artillery was to substitute soldiers for civilian drivers in 1800.

Still another influence of the old Neoclassical French army was the idea of army divisions, self-contained units of all arms and, in effect, miniature field armies of, say 10,000 men apiece, that could operate on their own for a time. The origin of the idea is traceable to Pierre de Bourcet, a French officer in the middle of the century who became interested in the possibilities of army divisions for operations in mountainous terrain. The French army conducted some tentative experiments with army divisions in the Seven Years' War, though the road system in Europe was not yet developed enough to make the idea practical. But between 1763 and 1789 the roads in western and central Europe were so improved in number and quality that the idea of a field army marching divided and fighting united became a real possibility. Once the mass army of the French Revolution appeared in the 1790s, it almost had to divide in order to forage efficiently, but its adoption of the army division also gave it a new flexibility for strategic maneuver, a capability that, of its generals, Napoleon in particular mastered. In 1800 Napoleon also solved the problem of span of control posed by too many army divisions by grouping them in army corps.

The defeats that the French national army inflicted on the Neoclassical armies forced change on them as well. After Napoleon's crushing victories over the old-style Prussian army at Jena-Auerstadt in 1806, military reformers such as Gerhard von Scharnhorst, August von Gneisenau, and Karl von Clausewitz helped to bring about innovations that by 1813 had made the Prussian army essentially a national force. Officers of the middle class no longer faced arbitrary limits on their promotions, there were many more of them in the army, and the men in the ranks included trained civilian reserves and militiamen. The field forces were organized along the new lines and were directed by a commander-in-chief assisted by a prototype modern general staff. To a lesser extent, the Austrian and Russian armies also made concessions to the new age, and when these armies, plus the Swedish, fought Napoleon's army at Leipzig in October 1813, some 430,000 men engaged in the Battle of the Nations, probably the largest battle ever fought to that time. Napoleon's defeat at Leipzig placed him on the road to his first abdication in April 1814.

Britain never tried to compete with France in raising numbers of troops during the Wars of the French Revolution and Napoleon, but it managed to nationalize its army by imposing compulsory militia duty within the British Isles and encouraging volunteers from the militia to enlist in the army for overseas duty. Britain also sought to use its army in theaters of war where it could be effectively supported by the superior British navy. Sir Arthur Wellesley, the later Viscount and Duke of Wellington, also developed a system of linear tactics that used terrain and light infantry to protect the line in such a way that it could beat back the attacks of the French columns.

Wellington's army usually took up a position on high ground which could not be easily outflanked, deployed its light infantry on the forward slopes in order to keep away the French skirmishers, and sheltered its infantry of the line, formed in two ranks, from French artillery behind the crest of the ridge. When the enemy's columns approached the crest, the thin red line delivered withering volleys before the French infantry could either close with the bayonet or form into line for firing. Wellington's system was displayed to best effect in his operations against the French in Spain and Portugal between 1807 and 1813. It was given a final test at the Battle of Waterloo in Belgium in June 1815 after Napoleon's return to power. Thanks to it, Wellington's army managed to hold off the French attacks until the Prussian army arrived to join in a final *coup de grâce* to Napoleon's fortunes.

# Epilogue

The wars of the American and French revolutions stand on the cusp between the older, more evolutionary patterns of war that had characterized civilization since its founding and the very rapid or revolutionary changes that have occurred in the last two hundred years. As great as the social-political impact on war produced by the revolutionary political upheavals of the late eighteenth century, the Industrial Revolution of the nineteenth century brought about even more rapid changes in war on land and sea.

At the end of the Napoleonic period, traditional shock action still played an important role on the battlefield, and a contemporary historian could even argue that an army like Alexander the Great's could have stood some chance of success against the armies of Napoleon or Wellington at Waterloo. [Arther Ferrill, *The Origins of War from the Stone Age to Alexander the Great* (New York and London: Thames and Hobson, Inc., 1985), p.217 and ff.] Within a few decades of 1815, such a claim would have been absurd. The coming of the Industrial Revolution and the mass production of muzzle-loading, rifled muskets gave infantry such tremendous defensive firepower that the day of the mass frontal attack with shock weapons such as the bayonet and saber was largely over. This fact was dramatized in blood by the great slaughters of attacking forces in the battles of the American Civil War (1861–1865). Similarly, the advent of the railroad upset traditional strategic assumptions about time, space, and logistics. At sea, naval warfare was given a new face with the advent of steam power, shell guns, armor protection, and mines.

Even before the end of the American Civil War, the rifled musket was being replaced by the even more deadly breech-loading rifle. The Franco-Prussian War (1870–1871) was the first in which the infantries of both sides were generally equipped with breech-loaders, and, in addition, the Prussian artillery was equipped with a breech-loading rifled cannon. Before the century was out, the infantry of Western armies were routinely equipped with repeating or magazine rifles capable of firing up to nine rounds with a single reloading, and a practical machine gun had appeared capable of firing four hundred rounds per minute. The new artillery was equipped with rapid-fire guns that could hurl high-explosive shells. By no coincidence, shell fire was the greatest cause of battlefield casualties in the First World War (1914–1918). At sea, the deadly toll was increased by combining the automotive torpedo with the submarine.

Western civilization was shaken by the destruction and loss of life occasioned by World War I, one in which the futility of massed frontal assaults against forces armed with the new firepower and protected by entrenchments was demonstrated over and over again. The introduction of poison gas merely intensified the near paralysis of the battlefield. In World War II new infantry tactics, mechanization, armored fighting vehicles, and close air support helped to overcome near paralysis on the battlefield, but by then great fleets of aerial bombers were able reach over surface forces to destroy whole cities systematically with high explosives and incendiaries. Famous old cities in Europe and Asia such as Coventry, Dresden, Berlin, Cologne, Shanghai, and Tokyo were largely reduced to rubble or blazing infernos between 1940 and 1945.

Urban extermination took a quantum leap forward in August 1945 when two atomic bombs destroyed Hiroshima and Nagasaki in the tick of a watch and thereby opened a new age in the patterns of war. To give a different twist to Winston Churchill's famous quotation, never before in the field of human conflict had so few slaughtered so many so quickly. The four decades and more since 1945 have only added to man's capacity for both mass and discrete destruction.

Yet the student should never lose sight of the fact that history is really a seamless garment and nothing in the present is wholly unconnected with the past. The theme of this book has been that each age had its own unique patterns of war produced by the reigning social-political, technological, and organizational factors of the time, and the differences in the patterns of war from one age to the next are important to understanding warfare at any given time. Still, this study also suggests that whatever the changes in the patterns of war, war itself always has been civilization's most unflattering handmaiden. Perhaps the most chilling of today's patterns is the capacity to destroy so much so cheaply, a pattern that threatens even the survival of the highly technical civilization which produces the weapons. Until humankind can find the means to solve the paradox between its propensity for civilized living and its ever-improving ability to destroy the civilization in which it lives, the study of the historical patterns of war, those distant as well as those more recently past, remains highly relevant to understanding how war and civilization became involved in this deadly embrace.

# SELECTED BIBLIOGRAPHY

Adams, Carol. *From Workshop to Warfare: The Lives of Medieval Women*. New York: Cambridge University Press, 1983.

Adcock, F. E. *The Greek and Macedonian Art of War*. Berkeley: University of California Press, 1957.

———. *The Roman Art of War Under the Republic*. Cambridge: Cambridge University Press, 1960.

Addington, Larry H. *The Patterns of War since the Eighteenth Century*. Bloomington: Indiana University Press, 1984.

Albion, R. G. *Forests and Sea Power: The Timber Problem of the Royal Navy, 1652–1862*. Hamden, Conn.: Archon Press, 1965.

Alden, John Richard. *The American Revolution, 1775–1783*. (*The New American Nation Series*.) New York: Harper and Row, Publishers, 1954.

Allmand, C. T., ed. *Society at War: The Experience of England and France during the Hundred Years' War*. New York: Harper and Row, 1973.

Anderson, Romola and R. C. Anderson. *The Sailing Ship*. New York: W. W. Norton and Company, 1963.

Andreski, Stanislav. *Military Organization and Society*. 2nd ed. Berkeley: University of California Press, 1968.

Asprey, Robert B. *War in the Shadows: The Guerrilla in History*. 2 vols. Garden City, N.Y.: Doubleday and Company, Inc., 1975.

Atkinson, Christopher T. *Marlborough and the Rise of the British Army*. New York and London: G. P. Putnam, 1921.

Ayalon, David. *Gunpowder and Firearms in the Mamluk Kingdom: A Challenge to a Medieval Society*. London: Valentine and Mitchell, 1956.

Bachrach, Bernard S. *Merovingian Military Organization, 481–751*. Minneapolis: University of Minnesota Press, 1972.

Bak, Janos M., and Bela K. Kiraly, editors. *From Hunyadi to Rakoczi: War and Society in Late Medieval and Early Modern Hungary*. New York: Brooklyn College Press, 1982.

Baker, Timothy. *The Normans*. New York: MacMillan and Co., 1966.

Barnett, Correlli. *Britain and Her Army, 1509–1970: A Military, Political, and Social Survey*. New York: William Morrow and Co., 1970.

Bass, George F., ed. *A History of Seafaring based on Underwater Archaeology*. New York: Wallace and Co., 1972.

Batchelor, John, and Ian Hogg. *Artillery*. New York: Ballantine Books, 1972.

Beeler, John. *Warfare in England, 1066–1189*. Ithaca, N.Y.: Cornell University Press, 1966.

———. *Warfare in Feudal Europe, 730–1200*. Ithaca, N.Y.: Cornell University Press, 1971.

Benedict, Ruth. *Chrysanthemum and the Sword*. New York and Scarborough: New American Library, 1974 [1946].

Bennett, Geoffrey. *Nelson the Commander*. New York: Charles Scribner's Sons, 1972.

Benson, Douglas S. *The Tartar War*. Chicago: Maverick Publications, 1981.

Bhakari, S. K. *Indian Warfare: An Appraisal of Strategy and Tactics of War in the Early Medieval Period*. New Delhi: Munshiram Manoharlal, 1981.

Boak, Arthur E. R., and William G. Sinnigen. *A History of Rome to A.D. 565*. 5th ed.

New York and London: The Macmillan Company and Collier-Macmillan Ltd., 1965.

Brodie, Bernard and Fawn. *From Crossbow to H-Bomb.* Rev. ed. Bloomington: Indiana University Press, 1973.

Bury, J. B. *A History of Greece to the Death of Alexander the Great.* London: Macmillan and Co., 1959.

Caesar, Julius. *The Battle for Gaul.* Translated by Anne and Peter Wiseman. Boston: David R. Godine, Publisher, 1980.

———. *The Conquest of Gaul.* Harmondsworth: Penguin Books, 1951.

Carter, John Marshal. *Arms and the Man: Studies in Roman and Medieval Warfare and Society.* Manhattan, Kansas: MA/AH Publishers, 1983.

Chambers, James. *The Devil's Horsemen: The Mongol Invasion of Europe.* New York: Atheneum, 1979.

Chandler, David. *The Art of Warfare in the Age of Marlborough.* New York: Hippocrene Books, 1976.

———. *The Campaigns of Napoleon.* New York: Macmillan and Co., 1966.

———. *Marlborough as Military Commander.* New York: Charles Scribner's Sons, 1973.

Churchill, Winston. *Marlborough, His Life and Times.* 6 vols. New York: Charles Scribner's Sons, 1933–1938.

Cipolla, Carlo M. *Guns, Sails, and Empires: Technological Innovation and the Early Phases of European Expansion, 1400–1700.* New York: Pantheon Press, 1965.

Clark, George. *War and Society in the Seventeenth Century.* Cambridge: Cambridge University Press, 1958.

Coggins, Jack. *The Fighting Man: An Illustrated History of the World's Greatest Fighting Forces through the Ages.* Garden City, N.J.: Doubleday and Company, Inc., 1966.

Cohen, Stephen P. *The Indian Army: Its Contributions to the Development of a Nation.* Berkeley: University of California Press, 1971.

Connolly, Peter. *Greece and Rome at War.* Englewood Cliffs, N.J.: Prentice-Hall, 1981.

Contamine, Philippe. *War in the Middle Ages.* Translated by Michael Jones. New York: Basil Blackwell, 1984.

Cornell, Tim, and John Matthews. *Atlas of the Roman World.* New York: Facts on File, 1987.

Corvisier, Andre. *Armies and Societies in Europe, 1494–1789.* Translated by Abigail T. Siddall. Bloomington and London: Indiana University Press, 1979.

Craig, Gordon A. *The Politics of the Prussian Army, 1640–1945.* New York: Oxford University Press, 1964.

Crankshaw, Edward. *The Fall of the House of Hapsburg.* New York: The Viking Press, 1963.

Dahmus, Joseph H. *Seven Decisive Battles of the Middle Ages.* Chicago: Nelson-Hall, 1983.

Davis, Burke. *The Campaign that Won America: The Story of Yorktown.* New York: Dial Press, 1970.

Delbruck, Hans. *History of the Art of War Within the Framework of Political History,* Vol. I, *Antiquity.* Translated by Walter J. Renfroe, Jr. Westport, Conn.: Greenwood Press, 1975.

———. *History of the Art of War Within the Framework of Political History,* Vol. III, *The Middle Ages.* Translated by Walter J. Renfroe, Jr. Westport, Conn. and London: Greenwood Press, 1982.

Diaz, Bernal del Castillo. *The Bernal Diaz Chronicles: The True Story of the Conquest of Mexico.* Translated and edited by Albert Idele. Garden City, N.Y., 1956.

Duffy, Christopher. *The Army of Frederick the Great.* London: Newton Abbot, 1974.

———. *Borodino and the War of 1812.* New York: Charles Scribner's Sons, 1973.

————. *Fire and Stone: The Science of Fortress Warfare, 1660–1860.* London: David and Charles, 1975.

————. *The Army of Maria Theresa.* London: Newton Abbot, 1977.

————. *Russia's Military Way to the West: Origins and Nature of Russian Military Power, 1700–1800.* London, Boston, and Henley on Thames: Routledge and Kegan Paul, 1981.

Dupuy, R. Ernest and Trevor N. Dupuy. *The Encyclopedia of Military History from 3500 B.C. to the Present.* Rev. ed. New York: Harper and Row, Publishers, 1977.

————, Trevor N. *The Evolution of Weapons and Warfare.* Indianapolis and New York: Bobbs-Merrill Company, Inc., 1980.

Dyer, Gwynne. *War.* New York: Crown Publishers, 1985.

Eggenberger, David. *An Encyclopedia of Battles: Accounts of Over 1,560 Battles from 1479 B.C. to the Present.* New York: Dover Publications, Inc., 1985 [1967].

Engels, Donald W. *Alexander the Great and the Logistics of the Macedonian Army.* Berkeley, Los Angeles, and London: University of California Press, 1978.

Ergang, Robert. *The Myth of the All-Destructive Fury of the Thirty Years' War.* Pocono Pines, Pa: Craftsman, 1956.

————. *The Potsdam Führer: Frederick William I, Father of Prussian Militarism.* New York: Columbia University Press, 1941.

Ferrill, Arther. *The Fall of the Roman Empire: The Military Explanation.* London and New York: Thames and Hudson, Inc., 1986.

————. *The Origins of War from the Stone Age to Alexander the Great.* London and New York: Thames and Hudson, Inc., 1985.

Finucane, Ronald C. *Soldiers of the Faith: Crusaders and Moslems at War.* New York: St. Martin's Press, 1983.

Fox, Robin Lane. *Alexander the Great.* London: Allen Lane, 1973.

Fuller, J. F. C. *A Military History of the Western World.* 3 vols. New York: Funk and Wagnalls Company, 1954–56.

————. *The Generalship of Alexander the Great.* London: Eyre and Spottiswoode, 1958.

Garlan, Yvon. *War in the Ancient World: A Social History.* Translated by Janet Lloyd. New York: W. W. Norton and Company, Inc., 1975.

Gaury, Gerald de. *The Grand Captain, Gonzalo de Cordoba.* London: Longmans, 1955.

Gibbon, Edward. *The History of the Decline and Fall of the Roman Empire.* 3 vols. London: Methuen, 1974 [1776–1788].

Gillingham, John, and J. C. Holt, editors. *War and Government in the Middle Ages.* Totowa, N.J.: Barnes and Noble Books, 1984.

Glover, Michael. *The Napoleonic Wars, 1792–1815: An Illustrated History.* New York: Hippocrene, 1978.

————. *Wellington as Military Commander.* New York: D. Van Nostrand Company, Inc., 1968.

Graham, Gerald S. *The Politics of Naval Supremacy: Studies in British Maritime Ascendancy.* New York: Cambridge University Press, 1965.

Grant, Michael. *The Army of the Caesars.* New York: Charles Scribner's Sons, 1975.

————. *The Twelve Caesars.* New York: Charles Scribner's Sons, 1975.

Grierson, Edward. *The Fatal Inheritance: Philip II and the Spanish Netherlands.* Garden City, N.Y.: Doubleday and Company, Inc., 1969.

Gush, George. *Renaissance Armies, 1480–1650.* Cambridge: Stephens, 1975.

Hackett, Sir John. *The Profession of Arms.* New York: Macmillan Publishing Company, 1983.

Halperin, Charles J. *Russia and the Golden Horde: The Mongol Impact on Medieval Russian History.* Bloomington: Indiana University Press, 1985.

Hamilton, Edith. *The Greek Way.* New York: Time Books, Inc., 1963 [1930].

Hawthorne, Daniel. *For Want of a Nail: The Influence of Logistics on War*. New York: Whittlesey House, 1948.

Hemming, John. *The Conquest of the Incas*. New York: Harcourt, Brace, and Jovanovich, 1970.

Hewitt, Herbert James. *The Organization of War under Edward III, 1338–62*. New York: Barnes and Noble Books, 1966.

Heymann, Frederick G. *John Ziska and the Hussite Revolution*. Princeton: Princeton University Press, 1955.

Higginbotham, Don. *The War of American Independence: Military Attitudes, Policies, and Practice, 1763–1789*. (*The Macmillan Wars of the United States*, edited by Louis Morton.) New York: The Macmillan Company, 1971.

Higham, Robin, ed. *Guide to the Sources of British Military History*. Berkeley: University of California Press, 1971.

Hindley, Geoffrey. *Medieval Warfare*. New York: Putnam, 1971.

Hittle, James D. *The Military Staff: Its History and Development*. Westport, Conn.: Greenwood Press, 1975 [1961].

Hoch, H. W. *Medieval Warfare*. New York: Crescent Books, 1983.

Hogg, Ian V. *Fortress: A History of Military Defense*. New York: St. Martin's Press, 1975.

Howard, Michael, editor. *The Theory and Practice of War*. Bloomington and London: Indiana University Press, 1965.

Howarth, David. *Trafalgar: The Nelson Touch*. New York: Aetheneum, 1969.

———. *Waterloo: Day of Battle*. New York: Aetheneum, 1968.

Hughes, Quentin. *Military Architecture*. London: Hugh Evelyn, 1975.

Humble, Richard. *Warfare in the Ancient World*. London: Cassell, 1980.

Hurley, Victor. *Arrows Against Steel: The History of the Bow*. New York: Mason/Charter, 1975.

Jones, Archer. *The Art of War in the Western World*. Urbana and Chicago: University of Illinois Press, 1987.

Keegan, John. *The Face of Battle: A Study of Agincourt, Waterloo, and the Somme*. New York: Vintage Books, 1977.

———. *The Mask of Command*. New York: Viking/Elisabeth Sifton Books, 1988.

Keller, Werner. *The Bible as History*. 2nd rev. ed. Translated by William Neil. New York: William Morrow and Company, Inc., 1981.

Kennedy, Paul. *The Rise and Fall of the Great Powers: Economic Change and Military Conflict from 1500 to 2000*. New York: Random House, 1987.

Kennett, Lee. *The French Armies in the Seven Years' War: A Study of Military Organization and Administration*. Durham, N.C.: Duke University Press, 1967.

Keppie, Lawrence. *The Making of the Roman Army: From Republic to Empire*. Totowa, N.J.: Barnes and Noble Books, 1984.

Kiernan, Frank A., Jr. and John K. Fairbank, eds. *Chinese Ways in Warfare*. Cambridge: Harvard University Press, 1974.

Kitchen, Martin. *A Military History of Germany from the Eighteenth Century to the Present Day*. Bloomington and London: Indiana University Press, 1975.

Koch, H. W. *Medieval Warfare*. London: Bison Books, 1978.

———. *The Rise of Modern Warfare, 1618–1815*. London: Bison Books, 1981.

Laffont, Robert. *The Ancient Art of Warfare: Antiquity, Middle Ages, Renaissance, 1300 B.C.-1650 A.D.* Greenwich, Conn.: New York Graphic Society, Ltd., 1966.

Lane, Frederic C. *Venice and History*. Baltimore: Johns Hopkins University Press, 1966.

Larrabee, Harold A. *Decision at the Chesapeake*. London: William Kimber, 1965.

Lawford, James, ed. *The Cavalry*. Indianapolis and London: Roxby Press and Bobbs-Merrill, 1976.

Lee, Stephen J. *Aspects of European History, 1494–1789.* 2nd ed. London and New York: Methuen, 1984.

Levy, Jack S. *War in the Great Power System, 1495–1975.* Lexington: University Press of Kentucky, 1983.

Lewis, Archibald R. *Sea Power and Trade in the Mediterranean,* A.D. *500–1000.* Princeton: Princeton University Press, 1951.

Lewis, Michael. *The History of the British Navy.* Harmondsworth: Penguin Books, 1957.

Liddell Hart, B. H. *Strategy: The Indirect Approach.* New York: Praeger, 1954.

Livy, *The War with Hannibal.* Translated by Aubrey de Selincourt and edited by Betty Radice. Harmondsworth: Penguin Books, 1965.

Lutwak, Edward N. *The Grand Strategy of the Roman Empire: From the First Century* A.D. *to the Third.* Baltimore and London: Johns Hopkins University Press, 1976.

Luvaas, Jay, ed. and trans. *Frederick the Great on the Art of War.* New York: Free Press, 1966.

MacMullen, Ramsay. *Christianizing the Roman Empire,* A.D. *100–400.* New Haven and London: Yale University Press, 1984.

Mahan, Alfred Thayer. *The Influence of Sea Power upon History, 1660–1783.* (American Century Series, edited by Louis M. Hacker). New York: Sagamore Press, Inc., 1957 [1890].

Mallett, Michael. *Mercenaries and Their Masters: Warfare in Renaissance Italy.* Totowa, N.J.: Rowman and Littlefield, 1974.

Maltby, William S. *Alba: A Biography of Fernando Alvarez de Toledo, Third Duke of Alba, 1507–1582.* Berkeley, Los Angeles, and London: University of California Press, 1983.

Marcus, G. J. *A Naval History of England: The Formative Centuries.* Boston and Toronto: Little, Brown, and Company, 1961.

———. *The Age of Nelson: The Royal Navy, 1793–1815.* New York: The Viking Press, 1971.

Marshall, S. L. A. *The Soldier's Load and the Mobility of a Nation.* Washington, 1950.

Massie, Robert K. *Peter the Great: His Life and World.* New York: Alfred K. Knopf, Inc., 1980.

Mattingly, Garrett. *The Armada* (The Sentry Edition). Boston: Houghton Mifflin Company, 1962.

May, Elemer C., Gerald P. Stadler, and John F. Votaw. *Ancient and Medieval Warfare.* Wayne, N.J.: Avery Publications Group, 1984.

McNeill, William H. *The Pursuit of Power: Technology, Armed Force, and Society since* A.D. *1000.* Chicago: University of Chicago Press, 1982.

Mitchell, Donald W. *A History of Russian and Soviet Sea Power.* New York: Macmillan Publishing Co., Inc., 1975.

Montgomery, Field Marshal Bernard L. *A History of Warfare.* Cleveland and New York: The World Publishing Company, 1968.

Nef, John U. *War and Human Progress.* Cambridge: Harvard University Press, 1950.

Oakeshott, R. Ewart. *The Archaeology of Weapons: Arms and Armor from Pre-history to the Age of Chivalry.* New York: Frederick A. Praeger, 1960.

Oman, Charles. *A History of the Art of War in the Middle Ages.* 2 vols. 2nd ed. New York: Benjamin Franklin, 1959.

———. *A History of the Art of War in the Sixteenth Century.* New York: E. P. Dutton and Co., Inc., 1937.

———. *The Art of War in the Middle Ages,* A.D. *378–1515.* Revised and edited by John Beeler. Ithaca, N.Y.: Cornell University Press, 1953.

O'Meara, Walter. *Guns at the Forks.* Pittsburgh: University of Pittsburgh Press, 1965.

Padfield, Peter. *The Battleship Era.* New York: David McKay Company, Inc., 1972.

Paret, Peter, ed. *Makers of Modern Strategy from Machiavelli to the Nuclear Age*. Princeton: Princeton University Press, 1986.

Parker, Geoffrey. *The Army of Flanders and the Spanish Road, 1567–1659*. Cambridge: Cambridge University Press, 1972.

———. *The Military Revolution: Military Innovation and the Rise of the West, 1500–1800*. Cambridge: Cambridge University Press, 1988.

———. *Spain and the Netherlands, 1559–1659: Ten Studies*. Short Hills, N.J.: Enslow Publishers, 1979.

———, ed. *The World: An Illustrated History*. New York: Harper and Row, Publishers, 1986.

Parker, H. M. D. *The Roman Legions*. Cambridge: W. Heffer and Sons, 1958.

———. *The Thirty Years' War*. London and New York: Routledge and Kegan Paul, 1967.

Parkman, Francis. *The Seven Years' War*. A Narrative taken from *Montcalm and Wolfe, The Conspiracy of Pontiac*, and *A Half-Century of Conflict*, edited by John H. McCallum. New York and Evanston: Harper and Row, Publishers, 1968.

Peckham, Howard H. *The Colonial Wars, 1689–1762*. (*The Chicago History of Civilization*, edited by Daniel J. Boorstin.) Chicago and London: The University of Chicago Press, 1964.

———, ed. *The Toll of Independence: Engagements and Battle Casualties of the American Revolution*. Chicago and London: The University of Chicago Press, 1974.

———. *The War for Independence*. (*The Chicago History of American Civilization*, edited by Daniel J. Boorstin.) Chicago: The University of Chicago Press, 1958.

Peterson, Harold L. *The Treasury of the Gun*. New York: Golden Press, 1962.

Potter, E. B., and Chester W. Nimitz. *Sea Power: A Naval History*. Englewood Cliffs, N.J.: Prentice-Hall, Inc., 1960.

Preston, Richard A. and Sidney Wise. *Men In Arms: A History of Warfare and Its Interrelationships with Western Society*. 4th ed. New York and London: Holt, Rinehart, and Winston, 1979.

Pritchard, James B., ed. *The Harper Atlas of the Bible*. New York: Harper and Row, Publishers, 1987.

Quick, John. *Dictionary of Weapons and Military Terms*. New York and San Francisco: McGraw-Hill Book Company, 1973.

Quigley, Carroll. *Weapons Systems and Political Stability: A History*. Washington, D.C.: University Press of America, 1983.

Quimby, Robert S. *The Background of Napoleonic Warfare*. New York: AMS Press, 1968 [1957].

Reynolds, Clark G. *Command of the Sea: The History and Strategy of Maritime Empires*. New York: William Morrow and Co., 1974.

Roberts, Michael. *Essays in Swedish History*. Minneapolis: University of Minnesota Press, 1967.

———. *Gustavus Adolphus: A History of Sweden, 1611–1632*. 2 vols. New York: Longmans, Green, 1953–1958.

———. *The Military Revolution, 1560–1660*. Belfast: Queen's College, 1956.

———. *Sweden's Age of Greatness, 1632–1718*. New York: St. Martin's, 1973.

Ropp, Theodore. *War in the Modern World*. Durham, N.C.: Duke University Press, 1959.

Roskill, Stephen W. *The Strategy of Sea Power: Its Development and Application*. London: Collins, 1962.

Ross, Steven. *From Flintlock to Rifle: Infantry Tactics, 1740–1866*. London: Associated University Presses, 1979.

Rothenberg, Gunther E. *The Art of Warfare in the Age of Napoleon*. Bloomington and London: Indiana University Press, 1978.

———. *The Military Border in Croatia, 1740–1881*. Chicago: University of Chicago Press, 1966.

Sanders, I. J. *Feudal Military Service in England*. Oxford: Oxford University Press, 1956.

Sarkar, Jaqadish Naravan. *The Art of War in Medieval India*. New Dehli: Munshiram Manoharlal, 1984.

Scheer, George F., and Hugh F. Rankin. *Rebels and Redcoats*. (*The New American Library*.) New York: Mentor, 1957.

Scullard, H. H. *Scipio Africanus: Soldier and Politician*. London: Thames & Hudson, 1970.

Sellman, Roger Raymond. *Medieval English Warfare*. New York: Roy Publishers, 1964.

Shy, John. *Toward Lexington: The Role of the British Army in the Coming of the American Revolution*. Princeton: Princeton University Press, 1965.

Stacey, C. P. *Quebec, 1759: The Siege and the Battle*. New York: St. Martin's Press, 1959.

Strachan, Hew. *European Armies and the Conduct of War*. London and Boston: Allen and Unwin, 1983.

Sun Tzu, *The Art of War*. Translated by Samuel B. Griffith. New York: Oxford University Press, 1963.

Symcox, Geoffrey, ed. *War, Diplomacy, and Imperialism, 1618–1763*. New York: Harper and Row, 1973.

Tarn, William W. *Alexander the Great*. 2 vols. Cambridge: Cambridge University Press, 1948.

Tuchman, Barbara W. *A Distant Mirror: The Calamitous 14th Century*. New York: Alfred A. Knopf, 1978.

Tunstall, Brian. *Admiral Byng and the Loss of Minorca*. London: P. Allan, 1928.

Turnbull, Stephen. *The Book of the Medieval Knight*. New York: Crown Publishers, Inc., 1985.

Turney-High, Harry Holbert. *Primitive War: Its Practices and Concepts*. 2nd ed. Columbia: University of South Carolina Press, 1971.

Vagts, Alfred. *A History of Militarism: Romance and Realities of a Profession*. 2nd ed. New York: Free Press, 1967.

Vale, Malcolm. *War and Chivalry: Warfare and Aristocratic Culture in England, France, and Burgundy at the End of the Middle Ages*. London: Duckworth, 1981.

Van Creveld, Martin. *Command in War*. Cambridge, Mass.: Harvard University Press, 1985.

———. *Supplying War*. Cambridge: Cambridge University Press, 1977.

———. *Technology and War: From 2000 B.C. to the Present*. New York and London: Collier MacMillan Publishers, 1989.

Verbruggen, J. F. *The Art of Warfare in Western Europe during the Middle Ages to 1340*. Translated by Sumner Willard and S.C.M. Southern. Amersterdam and New York: Elsevier/North Holland, 1977.

Warmington, B. H. *Carthage*. Baltimore: Pelican Books, 1960.

Warry, John. *Warfare in the Classical World: An Illustrated Encyclopaedia of Weapons, Warriors, and Warfare in the Ancient Civilisations of Greece and Rome*. London: Salamander Books, 1980.

Webster, Graham. *The Roman Imperial Army*. New York: Funk and Wagnalls, 1969.

Wedgwood, C. V. *The Thirty Years' War*. Harmondsworth: Pelican Books, 1958 [1937].

Williams, Eric. *From Columbus to Castro: The History of the Caribbean*. New York: Vintage Books, 1970.

Wintringham, Tom. *Weapons and Tactics*. Edited and updated by J. N. Blashford-Snell. Harmondsworth: Penguin Books, 1974.

Wise, Terrence. *Medieval Warfare*. New York: Hastings House, 1976.

Wolf, John B. *The Emergence of the Great Powers, 1685–1715.* New York: Harper, 1951.

Wood, Michael. *In Search of the Dark Ages.* New York and Oxford: Facts on File Publications, 1987.

————. *In Search of the Trojan War.* New York and Oxford: Facts on File Publications, 1985

Wright, Quincy. *A Study of War.* 2nd ed. Chicago: University of Chicago Press, 1965.

Yadin, Yagael. *The Art of Warfare In Biblical Lands in the Light of Archaelogical Study.* 2 vols. New York, Toronto, London: McGraw-Hill Book Company, Inc., 1963.

Young, Peter, and J. P. Lawford, eds. *History of the British Army.* London: Arthur Barker, Ltd., 1970.

# INDEX